Ecologies of Engaged Scholarship

T0351659

Story and auto-ethnography are study methods based on decolonizing and liberating research perspectives. Stories, auto-ethnographies, and other qualitative methodologies enable the researcher/educator to be both a research instrument and an object in their study. Stories allow for the examination of personal growth, its effect on practice, and their impact on community. The researcher/educator is able to witness her/his own life as they collaborate with participants. Through the use of story, auto-ethnography, and other qualitative methodologies, researchers/educators can link the history of self within their community/activist work to its present conditions as they map their collective community's future.

Ecologies of Engaged Scholarship explores the use of story and auto-ethnography as a tool to know 'self' and 'other' in relationship to capacity building, pedagogical processes, and activist scholarship. It highlights activist-scholarship to better understand the epistemology and landscape of activist research. Contributors to the book self-identify as activist-scholars or scholar-activists, and in their unique chapters they consider the values informing their work, the origins and nature of their work, and how they make meaning of their work. They also consider how family and/or community has been involved, how previous schooling experiences have affected their trajectory, and how particular relationships have worked to influence their philosophical understanding.

This book was originally published as a special issue of the *International Journal of Qualitative Studies in Education*.

Miguel A. Guajardo is a Professor in the Education and Community Leadership Program and a member of the doctoral faculty in School Improvement at Texas State University, USA. His research interests include issues of community building, community youth development, race and ethnicity, university and community partnerships, and Latino youth and families.

Francisco J. Guajardo is Professor of Organization and School Leadership and the Executive Director of the B3 Institute at the University of Texas Rio Grande Valley, USA. His research interests include school and community leadership, Latino epistemologies, borderlands studies, and the integration of the arts in community leadership.

Leslie Ann Locke is an Assistant Professor of Educational Policy and Leadership Studies at the University of Iowa, USA, and a Director of the Research Initiative on Social Justice and Equity. Her research interests include leadership for social justice, schooling for students from marginalized groups, equity-oriented education policy, and qualitative methodologies.

Ecologies of Engaged Scholarship

Stories from Activist Academics

Edited by
Miguel A. Guajardo, Francisco J. Guajardo and Leslie Ann Locke

Routledge
Taylor & Francis Group

LONDON AND NEW YORK

First published 2018 by Routledge

2 Park Square, Milton Park, Abingdon, Oxfordshire OX14 4RN
52 Vanderbilt Avenue, New York, NY 10017

Routledge is an imprint of the Taylor & Francis Group, an informa business

First issued in paperback 2019

British Library Cataloguing in Publication Data
A catalogue record for this book is available from the British Library

ISBN 13: 978-1-138-06328-0 (hbk)
ISBN 13: 978-0-367-26473-4 (pbk)

Typeset in Myriad Pro
by RefineCatch Limited, Bungay, Suffolk

Publisher's Note
The publisher accepts responsibility for any inconsistencies that may have arisen during the conversion of this book from journal articles to book chapters, namely the possible inclusion of journal terminology.

Disclaimer
Every effort has been made to contact copyright holders for their permission to reprint material in this book. The publishers would be grateful to hear from any copyright holder who is not here acknowledged and will undertake to rectify any errors or omissions in future editions of this book.

Contents

Citation Information

The chapters in this book were originally published in the *International Journal of Qualitative Studies in Education*, volume 30, issue 1–2 (January–February 2017). When citing this material, please use the original page numbering for each article, as follows:

Chapter 1
Editorial: An introduction to ecologies of engaged scholarship: stories from activist-academics
Miguel A. Guajardo, Francisco J. Guajardo and Leslie Locke
International Journal of Qualitative Studies in Education, volume 30, issue 1–2
(January–February 2017), pp. 1–5

Chapter 2
La Universidad de la Vida: *a pedagogy built to last*
Miguel A. Guajardo and Francisco J. Guajardo
International Journal of Qualitative Studies in Education, volume 30, issue 1–2
(January–February 2017), pp. 6–21

Chapter 3
Breaking into public policy circles for the benefit of underserved communities
Stella M. Flores
International Journal of Qualitative Studies in Education, volume 30, issue 1–2
(January–February 2017), pp. 22–31

Chapter 4
Living the consciousness: navigating the academic pathway for our children and communities
Kaiwipunikauikawēkiu Lipe and Daniel 'Bubba' Lipe
International Journal of Qualitative Studies in Education, volume 30, issue 1–2
(January–February 2017), pp. 32–47

Chapter 5
We help each other up: Indigenous scholarship, survivance, tribalography, and sovereign activism
Lee Francis IV and Michael M. Munson
International Journal of Qualitative Studies in Education, volume 30, issue 1–2
(January–February 2017), pp. 48–57

Chapter 6
I am, I am becoming: how community engagement changed our learning, teaching, and leadership
Matthew Militello, Marjorie C. Ringler, Lawrence Hodgkins and Dawn Marie Hester
International Journal of Qualitative Studies in Education, volume 30, issue 1–2
(January–February 2017), pp. 58–73

Chapter 7

Skipping toward seniority: one queer scholar's romp through the weeds of academe
Catherine A. Lugg
International Journal of Qualitative Studies in Education, volume 30, issue 1–2
(January–February 2017), pp. 74–82

Chapter 8

Finding my critical voice for social justice and passing it on: an essay
Leslie Ann Locke
International Journal of Qualitative Studies in Education, volume 30, issue 1–2
(January–February 2017), pp. 83–96

Chapter 9

Painting the emerging image: portraits of family informed scholar activism
Sophie Maxis, Christopher Janson, Rudy Jamison and Keon Whaley
International Journal of Qualitative Studies in Education, volume 30, issue 1–2
(January–February 2017), pp. 97–110

For any permission-related enquiries please visit:
http://www.tandfonline.com/page/help/permissions

Notes on Contributors

Stella M. Flores is an Associate Professor of Higher Education at the Steinhardt School of Culture, Education and Human Development at New York University, USA. In her research, she employs large-scale databases and quantitative methods to investigate the effects of state and federal policies on college access and completion rates for low-income and underrepresented populations.

Lee Francis IV is the Executive Director of Wordcraft Circle of Native Writers and Storytellers. The author's research interests are Indigenous stories, Indigenous education systems, and Indigenous organizational development.

Francisco J. Guajardo is Professor of Organization and School Leadership and the Executive Director of the B3 Institute at the University of Texas Rio Grande Valley, USA. His research interests include school and community leadership, Latino epistemologies, borderlands studies, and the integration of the arts in community leadership.

Miguel A. Guajardo is a Professor in the Education and Community Leadership Program and a member of the doctoral faculty in School Improvement at Texas State University, USA. His research interests include issues of community building, community youth development, race and ethnicity, university and community partnerships, and Latino youth and families.

Dawn Marie Hester is a program specialist for the Exceptional Children's Department with Pitt County School in Greenville, USA. She is a graduate of the Master of School Administration program at East Carolina University, USA.

Lawrence Hodgkins is the Assistant Principal at Riverside Middle School in Williamston, North Carolina, USA. He is currently a doctoral student at East Carolina University, USA.

Rudy Jamison is a Research Assistant at the University of North Florida, USA. He is pursuing his doctorial studies in Educational Leadership in the Department of Leadership, School Counseling and Sport Management. He earned a master's degree in Educational Leadership from the University of North Florida and a BS in Biology from Florida A&M University.

Christopher Janson is an Interim Chair and Associate Professor in the Department of Leadership, School Counseling and Sport Management at the University of North Florida, USA. He has published numerous works involving collective leadership, community leadership and development, and career, academic, and motivational development of urban school students.

Daniel 'Bubba' Lipe, PhD, is a registered Western Band Cherokee. His research and work focus on Traditional Ecological Knowledge and Western science. In particular he is interested in how the two knowledge systems are unique and also compatible, and how both knowledge systems can be utilized in the education system to prepare teachers who will shape the next generation of scientists to use multiple knowledge systems and worldviews to manage natural resources.

Kaiwipunikauikawēkiu Lipe, PhD, is currently a specialist faculty in Hawaiʻinuiākea School of Hawaiian Knowledge at UHM focusing on Native Hawaiian affairs. Her award-winning dissertation focused on the central question: How can UH Mānoa, a predominantly non-Hawaiian university, transform into a Hawaiian place of learning?

Leslie Ann Locke is an Assistant Professor of Educational Policy and Leadership Studies at the University of Iowa, USA, and a Director of the Research Initiative on Social Justice and Equity. Her research interests include leadership for social justice, schooling for students from marginalized groups, equity-oriented education policy, and qualitative methodologies.

Catherine A. Lugg is currently a Professor in the Department of Educational Theory, Policy and Administration at Rutgers University, USA. Her research interests include the politics of education, educational history, and queer politics.

Sophie Maxis is an Assistant Professor of School Counseling at the University of North Florida, Jacksonville, USA. Prior to completing her doctoral studies in Counselor Education from the University of Florida, Gainesville, she served as a secondary math teacher, a high school counselor, and with a university-school partnership for college-bound, first-generation college students.

Matthew Militello is the Wells Fargo Distinguished Professor in Educational Leadership at East Carolina University, USA. Prior to his academic career, Professor Militello was a public school teacher and administrator in Michigan.

Michael M. Munson is a PhD student at Montana State University, USA, and her research interests include Indigenous education, Indigenous community learning, and Indigenous education systems.

Marjorie Campo Ringler is an Associate Professor and Director of the Master of School Administration Program in Educational Leadership at East Carolina University, USA. Her areas of research include academic language proficiency, professional development, and instructional leadership.

Keon Whaley is a doctoral student and the 2014–2015 Eartha M. White Fellow at the University of North Florida, USA. He is a veteran, having served proudly and honorably in the United States Navy for six years. Upon completing military service, he studied Electronic Technology at Norfolk State University, earned a bachelor's degree in English, and a master's degree in Educational Leadership from the University of North Florida, respectively.

An introduction to ecologies of engaged scholarship: stories from activist-academics

This special edition of the *International Journal of Qualitative Studies in Education*, 'Ecologies of engaged scholarship: stories from activist-academics,' is a product of a distinct form of peer review journal production. 'Ecologies' captures an emerging epistemology of academic activism through a process congruent with the values and work the authors live by in their commitment to their respective communities, as they perform their privilege and agency for the public good. An invitation to participate was granted to a group of academics vetted by the editors, by senior scholars, and by other witnesses engaged in social change work. The edition has been produced through a community building process, as the guest editors convened the authors in rural South Texas in February 2015 to get-to-know each other and to think collectively about each of our stories as activist-academics. We came together a day before the start of the annual conference of the North Dakota Study Group, a national organization of progressive educators dedicated to advocacy of fair and appropriate teaching, learning, and evaluation practices. We spent three-and-a-half days building community: very purposefully, we broke bread together, shared stories, and established a level of trust where we could challenge each other as critical friends to find the stories that inspire us to engage in research, service, and teaching.

This developmental process did not begin with the preparation for the February get-together, nor did it start with the proposal to guest-edit this special edition. A more accurate origin for this volume takes us to our doctoral seminars at the University of Texas and at Texas A&M, when the three guest editors, at different times, sat in the classrooms of the respective colleges of education. Each of us can point to the significance of Jim Scheurich in our lives and to the importance of finding the interrelatedness between the concepts of scholarship, advocacy, and activism that took shape as we read, wrote, talked, and engaged with Jim as part of our graduate education. We can similarly point to key mentors such as Henry Trueba, Maenette Benham, Joe Feagin, our parents, and other non-academics from our communities who have shaped the foundation of our work. Our academic genealogy is the product of stories we share with them, and with so many more. And Scheurich has been key to this development – in ways he set up his classes, in ways he provoked, in ways he behaved. One of us recalls the day of a dissertation defense, when Jim stood up for a provocative argument one of us was making, and then reflected on the moment when he admittedly used his privilege. Jim said, 'Did you like the way I exercised my white privilege in your defense?' We love that candor, and the vulnerability that comes with it. Jim has taught us a great deal about privilege, especially white privilege. He and our mentors showed us how to use whatever privilege we have for the greater good. That's what this special edition is about. It is about using this place of privilege, the space that is a well-respected academic journal, to tell stories and to push for new ways of engaging scholarship and activism, and to push for ways of being as members of the academy.

The storytellers in this edition come from different geographical, classed, racial, and cultural upbringings. They come from the American Midwest, they come as Mexican immigrants into the US, they come from the Island of Oahu in Hawaii, they come from Native lands in the American Northwest, they come from Italian immigrants who settled in Michigan, they come from Haitian and African-American communities in Florida, they come from the Texas–Mexican borderlands, they come as South

American immigrants, and they come from Western European stock that has comprised the mainstream of American life during the past two centuries. The author list reflects both sides of the emerging and bridging landscape of the American demography, and the stories speak to the depth and breadth of the experiences that are cultural, racial, gendered, classed, epistemological, ontological, and axiological.

We turned the peer review process into a series of practices where we brought the authors together for an extended face-to-face gathering through which we nurtured a gracious space (Hughes, 2010) and then built a creative environment to explore the origins and meaning of our personal and collective activism. We are particularly sensitive to the production of auto-ethnography, to its introspective and deeply personal nature, and set out to establish a respectful and dignified process through which we could provide feedback to each other. The values of our individual and collective activism guide us to engage our work in this manner because this is how we work in community – with each other and for each other. When the work comes to life, it informs the decisions we make as we work for the public good.

Theory and ecologies of activist scholarship

Through these qualitative reflective essays, researchers link the history of self within their school and community/activist work to present conditions as they map their collective community's future. Authors use a method that best supports their story of development. Story and auto-ethnography are study methods based on decolonizing and liberating research perspectives proposed by, among others, feminist and post-colonial theorists Tuhiwai-Smith (1999), Moreton-Robinson (2000), Mohanty (2003), and Weiler (1988). These perspectives encourage studies in which the researcher becomes embedded in the lives of participants and engages actively in the political issues that inform their realities. These research perspectives give voice to participants, privilege the issues important to them, and explore practical applications of scholarship within participating communities, including the ecologies of self, organizations, and/or community (Guajardo et al., 2012).

We invited activist scholars to consider the philosophical understanding of the work they live. We invited them to pose questions such as: How are family and/or community involved in your work?; How do particular relationships you have cultivated through the years influence your activist work?; and How did your schooling experience affect your professional path? While we are interested in the stories of activist-academics, we believe these stories are not individualistic. We welcomed ethnographies that show movement away from the individualistic, or 'hero' story, toward a more collective consciousness, so encouraged authors to co-authored pieces.

We posed the following questions to participating activist scholars:

- How can we use stories and other forms of qualitative methods to witness our personal and the community's multidimensional growth?
- How can educators and/or researchers link an individual's and community's past to her/his/its present, and contribute to future perspectives?
- What innovations may be incorporated into the use and presentation of stories and other forms of qualitative research methods in schools, in communities, in higher education, and/or policy work?

When we convened the team to explore personal stories of activism and scholarship, to develop an emerging conceptual framework(s), and to engage the writing process, we used the theories and methods of activist scholarship to guide the conversations. The images below reflect that process and show symbolic representation of scholars' stories of activism. The peer review process of sharing, documenting, and developing each of the emerging documents was guided by a series of pedagogies including circle sharing, one-on-one conversations, public presentation, a gallery walk, and continuous feedback consistently communicated through *plática*, culturally expressive and nuanced form of conversation and inquiry (Guajardo & Guajardo, 2013). We share stories through a visual representation below, as they are situated in place.

Figure 1. Symbolic representation of activist work.

Though this text is mostly narrative, we employ visual and other multi-sensory strategies as tools for collection of observables, development of schemas, and presentation of stories (see Figure 1). The documents in this special edition are outlined below:

New Mexico Team: Two young indigenous scholars explore the role of sovereign scholarship, which fundamentally reorients the notions of qualitative scholarship from an indigenous perspective and utilizes traditional indigenous methodologies to explore the concepts of scholarship, activism, and the role of story.

Tennessee Member: A Chicana explores the ontological development of her activism as she shares the values, ontology, and pedagogies of a place-based agenda guided by the organic intellectuals in her family: her mother, father, grandmother, and siblings. Her ontological position explores why and how she lives her passion as her research informs a humane public policy agenda that largely focuses on recent immigrants, second language learners, their families, and their communities.

Mississippi/Iowa: A white woman explores the roots and process of her transformation as she grows into an activist scholar in search form equity for disenfranchised communities. She finds her energy in her working-class family and the struggles they share as she was growing up.

East Carolina: A team of faculty, students, and school leaders explore how community engagement has changed their teaching, learning, and leading in a principal preparation program, and in the lives of school leaders in rural schools in North Carolina.

Hawaii: Two indigenous scholars document their struggle of resistance and survival in a predominantly white institution that sits on indigenous lands. Their activist scholarship intersects intergenerational education and cultural revitalization with elders and children alike.

Texas: Two brothers document the pedagogies of their father through stories that expound upon values, ontology, epistemology, and identity formation. Their story begins at their father's funeral, and proceeds through a reflective process that highlights the intersections of an old school education of an organic intellectual with their work in higher education. This learning informs their activist-academic work.

Florida: A diverse group of scholars, students, and community activists describe how the frame of family both informs and is informed by their collective activism. The authors share individual and collective stories exploring efforts to orient their community work away from the transactional nature of the academy, and toward developmental relationships first learned in family.

New Jersey: This reflective essay, which is both autobiographical and historical in nature, is framed by answering the following questions posed by the editors:

(a) What is your work and what values inform it? (b) How do you do this work? (c) Why do you do this work, i.e. to what end?

The author's response:

> I suspect some of the readers will be disconcerted by my observations and experiences, but to some extent, that is precisely the point. If you are going to engage in social justice issues as part of your larger research agenda, you must become what Michael Eric Dyson calls, 'a privileged pest.' Those of us who are professors, particularly those of us at major research institutions, have enormous class privileges. These are then compounded if we are white, non-queer, and/or male, etc. (see Hutchinson, 1997; Valdes, 1995). We can control the nature of our labor, at least somewhat, and if we are ferociously persistent, we can see the fruits, or in my case, the fruity fruits of our labor.

Impact of research

This research expands the understanding of activist research through the stories of scholars who work on a variety of issues and who come from different walks of life. This edition provides real-life examples of activist research and how it transforms teaching, service, and research. It enhances the literature of an emerging activist ontology and epistemology that informs a new frontier of activist scholarship.

References

Guajardo, F., & Guajardo, M. (2013, Fall). The power of Plática. *Reflections: A Journal of Public Rhetoric, Civic Writing, and Service Learning, 13*, 159–164.

Guajardo, M., Guajardo, F., Oliver, J., Valadez, M. M., Henderson, K., & Keawe, L. O. (2012). A conversation on political imagination and advocacy for educational leadership. *UCEA Review, 53*(3), 19–22.

Hughes, P. (2010). *Gracious space: A practical guide to working better together*. Seattle, WA: Center for Ethical Leadership.

Hutchinson, D. L. (1997). Out yet unseen: A racial critique of gay and lesbian legal theory and political discourse. *Connecticut Law Review, 29*, 561–645.

Mohanty, C. T. (2003). *Feminism without borders*. London: Duke University Press.

Moreton-Robinson, A. (2000). *Talkin' up the white women: Aboriginal women and feminist*. St. Lucia, Qld: University of Queensland Press.

Tuhiwai-Smith, L. (1999). *Decolonizing methodologies: Research and indigenous peoples*. New York, NY: Zed Books Ltd.

Valdes, F. (1995). Queers, sissies, dykes, and tomboys: Deconstructing the conflation of "sex", "gender", and "sexual orientation" in Euro-American law and society. *California Law Review, 83*, 3–377.

Weiler, K. (1988). *Women teaching for change*. Westport, CT: Bergin & Garvey Publishers.

Miguel A. Guajardo
Francisco J. Guajardo
Leslie Ann Locke

La Universidad de la Vida: a pedagogy built to last

Miguel A. Guajardo and Francisco J. Guajardo

ABSTRACT

This article weaves the life of a Mexican laborer, who with his wife brought his family to the United States and mentored two university professors, as they became activists in their craft. The professors honor their father through a reflective process where they share and make sense of a series of stories that describe their Papi's experience in La Universidad de la Vida. The narratives speak to ontology of research, the utility of stories, particularly as stories can shape identity, capture critical life moments, and can help us make meaning of lived experiences, a methodology not commonly explored in education research.

Introduction and context

Our activist academic work is first and foremost grounded in our brotherhood, as we are separated by only a little more than a year, and we both had the profound privilege of being raised by loving parents and a caring community. Secondarily, our work as academics is a hybrid approach grounded in pedagogy of place, identity formation, and asset building negotiated through a process that pays careful attention to history and context. Mentors from different walks of life have privileged us with wisdom, passion, and languages. As second language learners we have experienced the perpetual game of 'catch up,' continuously grappling with the English language and trying to understand the values of the dominant culture and its institutions. Along the way, we made the decision to stop playing 'catch up.' This occurred before we arrived in academia, when we were high school teachers and community activists. As we entered academia, we were drawn to Trueba's pedagogy of hope (1999, 2004), Freire's concept of awareness and critical consciousness (1998, 2000, 2002), Valenzuela's politics of cultural caring (1999), Ah Nee-Benham's identity and indigeneity (1998; Ah Nee-Benham & Cooper, 2000), Scribner's micropolitics (1999), Scheurich's coloring epistemology (1997), Reyes' embedded mentoring (1999), and Delgado Bernal's pedagogies of everyday life of Chican@s (2006). These mentors and their work influence our professional identity, but what we do is inspired most deeply by our parents and their life stories. This essay takes the reader on a genealogical trip through the spaces and stages of our formation, as it examines our identity and work as professors. This is a genealogy of stories that tell how we have been shaped by individual and collective action in relationship with numerous people present in our lives, the ecologies they bring with them, and most importantly the social DNA given by our parents that spelled a compelling commitment to education and community.

A series of stories about our greatest mentor, our father, guides this autoethnography that is interdependent and relational in nature. The stories are raw and authentic. We refer to him as our father, or Papi; same with our mother, who we call Mami. The structure and rhythm call for storytelling, followed by critical self-reflection to make sense of the story. We invite you to do the same, and encourage you to not get stuck in the story, but to see it as a mechanism through which to explore your own journey. We invite researchers and academics who might live on the margins to find themselves within these spaces of resistance, resilience, and struggle as we collectively develop a pedagogy and epistemology of the self within our ecology. We have come to appreciate this experience for what it does to students in our classrooms, and for the impact it has in our communities. Our research teaches us that pedagogies that encourage the exploration of the self within their particular ecologies of knowing are transformational for school leaders. We invite the reader to see these stories as circular, rather than linear. We organize the text through identification of critical moments to demonstrate impact in our development as sons, brothers, students, community builders, teachers, fathers, and researchers.

Our brand of activism mirrors our father's public actions. He was radical by definition, and thereby changed his life, changed his family, changed his community. He was a man of private action, not of public demonstration. He was different than anyone we have known in his willingness to give: wisdom, energy, time, humor, love, and whatever was needed to help. This was his gift to us, and to the world. Through this essay, we can only attempt to mimic his actions, as we tell stories that have shaped who we are as public people and activist academics. In Papi's mind, the little things were important; dignity and humility were essential in shaping the public person. Like him, we work to change our lives, to change the lives of others, and to change organizations and communities. This change is grounded in and informed by a micropolitical action that is at work every day. It is the commitment to get up daily and do the right things for us, for our families, and for the public good. This is the lesson of our father, who taught us a pedagogy built to last.

How to say *adiós* (good bye)

When our father died, we shared a video at the funeral from an oral history we conducted with him five years earlier. In the video, he responded to the question: *Cómo quieres ser recordado*? ('How do you want to be remembered?') His answer appeared as if he were engaged in a *plática* with those who came to pay respects. He posed questions, he reflected on events, he generously spread wisdom, and he did so as if speaking to multiple audiences: the camera, his children, the community, and posterity. Most directly, he said he wanted to be remembered as someone who had been *cumplido*. To translate *ser cumplido* is to describe a heightened state of being. It means to have integrity, to be someone who can be counted on, and to show fidelity to the things one commits to. In his easy conversational way, he told the community how he wanted to be remembered, and by extension he encouraged everyone in attendance to *ser cumplidos, y que hagan por el próximo* (to be committed and generous to each other). Our work as university professors stems from that direct piece of wisdom our father shared at his funeral and is derived from the life we saw him live.

This essay is an opportunity to honor our father's life, and to reflect on the enduring influence he had on us as emerging academics, and as activist professors who learned from the life he modeled. He was the quintessential mentor. He exercised a poetic quality that manifested itself until his last day, when he waited to take his last breath on his birthday. José Ángel Guajardo died 19 May 2013, when he turned 77, after a long battle with lung cancer. He lived a life of purpose, and he reflected on the purpose in an engaging and perpetual way. The frequent *pláticas* he shared with us, typically over *un cafecito*, were things of beauty, as he curiously asked about our work, our travels, our own purpose. He was born in a rural village in northern Mexico, lived an early life as a goat-herder, sojourned north of the international border in his late teens in search of temporary work in South Texas, but returned to Mexico every time. He married our mother in 1959 in the state of Tamaulipas, and they brought the family to the United States in the late 1960s.

As brothers we reflect deeply on his life through modalities that include our own journaling, an autobiography our father wrote, ethnographic accounts we have produced, an elongated oral history we conducted with him, and numerous other stories that give shape to him and the family narrative. He did not have much formal schooling, though he was intensely proud of his fourth-grade education in a rural school in the village of San Felipe, Nuevo León, in northern Mexico. The school did not offer a fifth grade, so he repeated the fourth grade twice; it's how much he loved school. We learned a great deal about our father because he raised us with stories, and shared numerous *anécdotas,* as he called them in the title of his autobiography (Guajardo, 1988). The *anécdotas* covered a wide autoethnographic range: from his early childhood, to his adolescence, to his adult life. We had a front row seat as witnesses to his life as a Mexican immigrant father and husband, and we sought him out for counsel at every step of our formative experiences. Shortly after he penned his autobiography, which he wrote upon our request, we engaged him in an oral history that includes no less than a dozen installments. From one of those installments, we took footage to use at his funeral.

It was surreal as relatives, friends, neighbors, and acquaintances walked into the funeral home and heard our father's voice with crisp clarity. 'He's here,' said one friend. Funerals incubate a host of human emotion. Some in attendance felt relief, because Papi's suffering had ceased. Others felt loss. There was great anxiety, too. When the video played, Papi's voice calmed the collective anxiety. The video was a product of our personal interest to know more, but it was also the result of our instincts as researchers (Patton, 2002). Showing the video was an act of engagement, where our father could have a *plática* with the community, where he could help friends and family understand how to remember him, and where he could help them move on with their lives. So, the friend was correct. Papi was there, still teaching, still mentoring. He taught us that *pláticas* were critical for educational purposes. Through *pláticas* came stories. This was also an exercise in reciprocity, as we took the research and presented back to relatives, friends, and the community at large. Through the stories in the video, Papi demonstrated the commitment to his family, to his friends, and to his community. Those relationships fueled his spirit, guided his public service, and revealed his public pedagogy. We felt compelled to use our research to help our father say his last public good-bye, so he could deliver yet another lesson before leaving. As Behar wrote, it became an anthropology that breaks the heart (1996).

Ser cumplido

When we were four and five years old, respectively, our parents decided to make the move from Río Bravo, Tamaulipas, to the United States. One day in the fall of 1968, Papi took us to Monterrey in the neighboring state of Nuevo Leon to apply for legal residence through the Mexican Consulate (see Figure 1). The federal office was housed in a two-story building, and our father went into a room on the second floor to present his application and to sit for an interview. We stayed outside the office, waiting, and playing; perhaps more accurately, we 'horsed around.' Our play soon turned rough, and we found ourselves rolling down the stairway from outside the Consulate's office to the base of the stairway on the first floor.

About the time our downward rolling stopped, Papi stepped out of the office, which we clearly detected when we looked up as we lay on the floor. More worrisome, however, was his countenance – he did not look happy. Without hesitation, our father made his way down to us. His form of discipline was about to be exacted, when he was interrupted by a stranger who simultaneously approached us, apparently to help us off the floor. The stranger also spoke to our father, and as he did so, pre-empted the on-the-spot discipline our father would've assuredly dispensed. The man introduced himself as Polo Medrano, and asked our father, 'How was your interview?' Papi responded that his application for legal residency to the United States had been rejected. What happened next was a series of events where Polo Medrano helped our family immigrate to the United States. He and his wife Amelia even offered housing to our family for several months, so that our parents could earn and save enough to find a permanent place to live.

The Medrano family moved to Oregon in the early 1970s, and through the years our parents kept up with them through the occasional phone call and a few personal visits when the Medranos traveled to Texas. In 2010, Amelia died of cancer, and on her deathbed, she asked Polo for a personal favor. She reminded Polo of the girl who had been his girl friend, before she and Polo had met and fallen in love. She told Polo that she knew the girl had never married and asked him to find her, and if she agreed, to

Figure 1. José Angel with three older sons, fall 1968.

resume their relationship. Polo agreed he would, and within a year after Amelia's death, Polo married his old girlfriend.

Papi told us this story one morning over coffee, when we asked him what had become of Polo and Amelia. He told us Polo lived in Mexico, where he had found his new wife. When asked why he hadn't brought her to Texas, he said Polo was working through the immigration process for his wife. She was a Mexican national, and it cost several thousand dollars to pay the application fee to bring her into the country legally. But Polo didn't have the money, and the bank would not give him a loan because Polo did not have established credit. So our father explained that he had taken out a loan himself and had given the money to Polo, so he could bring his new wife to Texas. *Están esperando la carta de inmigración* (They're waiting for the letter from immigration), he said.

At the time, our father was on a fixed income, primarily living on a monthly Social Security check. When he told us the story of the loan, we asked why he hadn't asked us for the money. We told him we would be happy to help. But our father explained that it was his responsibility to repay Polo for the generosity he offered that fateful day in Monterrey, as they met while the two of us lay on the floor. He reminded us that Polo had helped us get into the US, had given us refuge, and had been a kind friend. He said that he had to *cumplir con* Polo.

Since we were undergraduates at the University of Texas at Austin, we have volunteered in our hometown in the Rio Grande Valley. We formalized the work and brought other local partners into it through founding a non-profit named the Llano Grande Center for Research and Development (LGC), an organization that allows us to harness and scale up the work. The most important source of inspiration is the commitment to *cumplir*, the social responsibility of giving back to the community inculcated by our parents. This has informed our work as teachers, community builders, researchers and activists. *Cumplir* is at the core of our ontology as activist academics; it serves as a guidepost. It is what we teach our children and our students. But to *cumplir* is often at odds with the impulse of the institution, which is often to pursue self-serving activities or to compete for the big grants. How to approach the dictates of the academy warrants continual negotiation, but it is negotiation guided by core values. In our case, it is guided by the need to *cumplir*.

La Universidad de la Vida

We knew Papi as a compulsive note-taker. He kept a notepad to keep track of bills he paid. He kept one where he noted significant events, people, celebrations, and funerals. He and Mami never missed a funeral; being there when others most needed comfort was important to them. He started another notepad in the early 1960s that recorded every job he took on. He worked on that notepad until the day he retired as an elementary school janitor with the local school district. He often pointed to his 45-year record of employment, where he never missed a day of work, save for the days when he underwent major surgery – and the recovery, of course. During the four-and-a-half decades of his formal work span, he was also never jobless, and he was very proud of that. In an understated way, he made sure we knew. But his notepad only contained notes, no narratives.

While undergraduates at the University of Texas, we asked our father if he had written some of the stories he and our mother told as part of how they raised us. We told him the stories had had such value as guideposts for living the right kind of life, and they were an integral part of our emerging identity. He said he had not, but by end of the year – that was 1986 – he turned his notepads into narratives, and completed the first installment of his autobiography, which he entitled *Anécdotas de mi Vida* (Guajardo, 1988). Through the exercise, he explained that he had become a more reflective storyteller, as he trans-formed his notes into stories, or *anécdotas*, as he liked to call them. One of his signature *anécdotas* is a treatise on the process of his education. He recalled the richness of his early years in the rural school in San Felipe, but he mostly focused on the critical nature of life experience as his core curriculum. The most critical lessons learned, he learned through experience. When we became teachers, we had thus been told by our father of the significance of lived experience as an important part of personal and professional development. Papi came to understand his life experience as the best schooling, and he described the process as his *Universidad de la Vida* (The University of Life).

Papi had a fourth-grade education, and our mother had no formal schooling. But they were both *bién educados*. Valenzuela (1999) and other Mexican American scholars use the Spanish term *educación* to highlight the difference between being schooled and being respectful and honorable. To be *bién educado* is a significant cultural acknowledgment, even accomplishment. It means one has achieved mastery of respectful and gracious behavior. It means one speaks to elders in a respectful manner, and communicates in Spanish in the presence of Mexicano elders. This has been a persistent tension that has kept us grounded, particularly during times when we thought we were real smart. Like the time one of us was knee-deep in dissertation writing, engulfed in books, and isolated from the outside world. When our father paid a visit, he looked at all the books, the laptop on which the dissertation was being written, and said, *mijo, lo más educado, lo más pendejo* (Son, the more educated, the more stupid you become.) The context was that our mother had gotten sick, because one of us had not visited her in weeks. *Éso, es ser mál educado*, (That is not being *educado*) was our father's critique. Looking after our mother was a basic measure of being *bién educado*. On occasions when we came back home during semester breaks at the university, our father would keep us in check, particularly if we did not meet the *educado* standard. When he detected a slip in our cultural competence, he would pose the question: *de que les sirve la educación?* (What good is your education?)

Papi learned the metric of *educación* through his experience in the *Universidad de la Vida*. His curric-ulum was life experience, and his organic forms of accountability proved a critical complement to our university education. His *Universidad de la Vida* teachings added important texture and humanity to the process of our educational development, and to our identity as emerging educators. *En Casa Guajardo*, to be *bién educado* was also a form of resistance. It was a way our parents ensured we maintain the Spanish language, the way we understood and respected the ways of the *barrio*. Like a modern day

Vygotsky (1978), our father used the zone of proximal development to scaffold the necessary litera-cies of life and order of the world. He understood issues of power, but he also knew how to negotiate these spaces through a set of pedagogical tools. He needed his sons to know the value of hard work, the utility behind saying please and thank you, and the wisdom to know when to walk away from unhealthy conflict – the latter has saved our careers several times. This brand of education has gifted us the ability to engage in meaningful and sustained conversations with community partners, who in their own context and culture are *bién educados*.

The parable of Pablito

Our father established a number of rituals intended as part of our upbringing: the regular visits to rela-tives, the weekly trips into Rio Bravo for a haircut, and the regular reading of Pablito's story. One of our father's most prized possessions was his library, a collection of old books he kept from his school years in San Felipe. There was the book on geography that he often cited, the science book, the math book. But the book on *civismo* (civics) was his favorite. That book had the story of Pablito, a parable that would be etched in our collective consciousness. He would gather his four sons around him to deliver his best rendition of the story of *la escuela rural*, where the protagonist was a Mexican boy named Pablito. The boy grew up in the village, just like our father had, and he helped the family economy through goat and sheepherding. Pablito loved his school and his village, and upon completing all the grades at the school decided to leave the rural community to continue his education. He spent years studying in the big city and often thought about the rural village he loved so dearly. Pablito soon finished his studies in the city, and he had a decision to make. When Papi read this during our younger years, he would pause at this point in the story to ask what we thought would happen next.

Two things happened next in this story: (1) Pablito returned to his rural home, and (2) he came back with skills to help develop the village. That became the point of the story, but the moral was in our father's interpretation. Pablito's decision was the definition of acting for the public good. He became educated so he could help himself, yes, but the way our father saw it, the higher calling was to help the village. The story, how it was directed and acted by our father, and the frequency and persistence of the performance became a central part of how we were raised. A measure of its effectiveness is evidenced in how all four brothers became educated, and all came back to help develop our community – in one way or another.

This was our navigational tool, our moral and academic compass, and what has informed our research agenda. If this is what was important to the most important man in our lives, it was what would be important to us. The process is clearly more complicated than this facile analysis of the story, but the point is that the foundation was set, and the space and place where we would give back was defined. Our research became about this place that raised us, the issues that shaped us, and the challenges our community faces daily. Pablito's story showed us that through education and the process of breaking out of our own isolation, we could change the world around us. The cycle of development played true in the stories of Pablito and continues to play true today. The people in our world and the places we have lived influence our ontology and epistemology as researchers. They form our research agenda that is grounded in practice and that pays attention to voices closest to the issues. This agenda is collaborative in nature, and is guided by the public good.

This research carries a different responsibility that academia may not see as important. Like Pablito, our impact is measured in multiple ways – through a focus on community, by the number of people who read and discuss the work, and by the lives that are changed as a result. Which peer reviewed journal we publish in, or what the acceptance rate may be, are not the most important measures we look at. Neither the fictional Pablito, nor the real character that was our father would consider academic journals as the most authentic measures. Pablito's narrative of education for community change is the standard, the foundation on which our work as teachers, researchers, and community builders is based. Pablito's story shaped our lives, guides our work, and has changed our community. It informs the research methods our students employ in their work, both in graduate school and in their communities.

'Si es veterano, no es veterano'

Our parents curated their living room walls with family photographs, memorabilia of their children and grandchildren, a shrine adorned by university diplomas of the Guajardo boys, a variety of Virgens of Guadalupe. And then there was the wood carved portrait of Papi in military uniform (see Figure 2). The wooden image commemorated his time in mandatory 'marching camp,' a rite of passage for every able bodied young man during the post-Revolutionary time in twentieth-century Mexico. The older among us, Miguel, understood the story of that wooden picture from an early age, but for some reason one of us did not get the real story, until an experience we had in 1974 in Holland, Michigan.

Our family became part of the migrant farm-working stream during the spring of 1974. The destination was a labor camp in Keeler, Michigan, and strawberry fields in and around Van Buren County. We arrived in April and found snowing, winter-like weather, which meant we could not work until the weather improved. Our modest resources would not last long, so our father went looking for other work, and for assistance to make ends meet. Every place he went, he took us, or our older brother Pepe, to help translate, because our father did not know English, and we quickly realized most local Michiganders did not know Spanish. We made a stop with our father at the food stamps office in Holland, where the social worker that tended to our food stamps application did not know Spanish, so the two of us were pressed into translation duty. We deftly handled questions such as name, address, date of birth, and ages of the children. But the question, 'Are you a veteran, Mr. Guajardo?' elicited split responses. The give-and-take went something like this:

Miguel: 'No, my father is not a veteran.'

Francisco: 'Yes, he is! Remember the wooden picture at the house? He's in a soldier's uniform. He's a veteran!'

Figure 2. José Angel in wood carved image, ca. 1957.

So we turned to our father: *Papi, el señor quiere saber que si eres veterano de guerra*? (The man wants to know if you're a war veteran?) Papi confirmed that he was not, and he asked why the confusion. When we told him the source of the debate, he broke out in laughter, then composed himself and said, *Díganle al señor que no soy veterano, pero que sí marché, cómo fué mi deber cómo Mexicano*. (Tell the gentleman I am not a veteran, but I did March as part of my national duty in Mexico.)

The *veterano* experience became one of Papi's favorite stories. He laughed heartily every time he told it, but it was an intriguing laughter, as our father was wont to have fun with stories. He found stories to be a vital source of social and cultural transmission. Related to the *veterano* story, he expressed joy at how funny the moment was, celebrated our innocence, and recognized the weighty responsibility we assumed as brokers of important family moments. At prepubescent ages, we were in the middle of negotiating labor contracts with Anglo farmers, filled out medical applications and translated and interpreted communication with nurses, doctors, and other health professionals, and even debated whether our father was a veteran of a foreign war. Our parents trusted us as we engaged in all these functions. Though they must have been humbled by the experiences, they never showed weakness; to the contrary, they were elegant and nurturing in giving us the space to exercise our own agency as sons, and as valuable members of the family. This is an important source of our strength.

We were raised in the borderlands, a playground that nurtures the imagination (Anzaldúa, 1987). We were gifted with two languages, negotiated different cultures, and learned which knowledge and language were valued in given situations (González, Moll, & Amanti, 2005). Life along the border is about contextual and dynamic spaces. In these spaces our parents needed us, and we needed them. A critical skill set our parents developed was the ability to negotiate the shifting variables of culture, institution, home, and language. They were the original social constructivists in our lives. They adapted to their surroundings in ways that were dignified, respectful, and as it turns out, sustainable (Guajardo & Guajardo, 2002, 2004, 2008). They listened to us as school children and valued our knowledge as we brought academic and other life experiences into the home. They listened to us when we were introduced into the sometimes-violent world of sports in high school, when we went to college, when we became teachers. Listening to their children was something they took seriously. Our parents then lived and learned vicariously when we began to travel the world. They always worried when we traveled and demonstrated deep curiosity upon our returns. Our father reminded us of the first time he saw a train, when he ran to hide behind *Abuelita* Virginia, frightened of this strange iron machine. When we grew up, he was happy to see the world through our own travels.

As our parents shifted their ways of being based on lived experiences, they frequently engaged us in conversations on understanding power dynamics. Our father's frame of reference was as a laborer, our mother's as a housewife, but they knew abundantly from the relationships they had experienced through family, community, and work. They taught us that without dignity and respect, power could be a very violent thing. They gave us the power to make important decisions when necessary and trusted us unconditionally. We wrote checks for them, translated and interpreted language for them, and when they were not around we negotiated this power with each other. We were not always right, and like the *veterano* story, we were often hilariously wrong, but we always felt supported. The range of experiences constitutes the core of our development process as teachers, researchers, and activists.

Building *el barrio*

Two years after arriving from Mexico, our parents got a tip from Toñita Rodríguez, an elderly woman from our new hometown of Elsa. Toñita looked after people, especially families that were just looking for a break. Our family appeared to meet the criteria, and as someone who understood systems, Toñita suggested to our parents that we apply for federal housing, otherwise known as *Los Proyectos*, or the Projects. We did, and in the summer of 1971, we moved into 302 West 3rd Street in Elsa, a federal housing apartment where we would live for the next eight-and-a-half years. In return, Toñita earned the loyalty and life-long friendship from our family. Years later, her grandkids would become our students at the high school, and we made sure to help them get into good colleges. Toñita taught our parents how to look for opportunities in this new country and showed them how to navigate their new environment. We taught her grandchildren how to do the same.

Growing up in the Projects was magical. Our parents fit the old model of the gendered spheres of influence, as our father worked outside the home, behaved as the public face and voice of the family, and often engaged in political and other public discourse with guests and with those we visited. Our mother administered domestic duties, offered the preponderance of the nurturing, and looked after the day-to-day activity of the kids inside and outside the home. As Papi modeled the gainful employment outside the home, Mami managed our leadership development, particularly in relation to our interaction with the dozen or so other youth from the neighborhood, or what we referred to as *el barrio*. By the time we were eight and nine, we were organizing our own baseball league during the summer, football games during the fall, basketball in the winter, and *canica* (marbles) and *trompo* (tops) tournaments year round. We salvaged throw-away sticks as baseball bats, old tire rims as basketball hoops, shared gloves and other equipment, and even carved the base paths for the make-shift baseball field with hoes borrowed from a neighbor. All the while, Mami (and other neighboring mothers) made sure everyone was safe, and well-fed. She offered advice when needed and ensured conditions were ripe so that kids in the *barrio* could play and grow up in happy and healthy ways. Mami supervised this leadership development process and allowed us the space to navigate our own world.

After about five years living in the projects, our parents began to think about the eventuality of moving out. The Housing Authority director often spoke of the purpose of federal housing as an opportunity to help families during times of need, but with the intent to also help families move into home ownership, at some point. Our parents listened carefully, and they looked around the area and found an affordable lot in a *colonia* (unincorporated community) outside of Elsa, just a few miles from the Projects. They gave a down payment, a nominal amount according to Papi's records, on an acre of land and began their monthly payments on a 10-year loan from the property owner – our father documented every payment in one of his notepads. When the director of the Projects raised our monthly rent by over 300%, we made the move to our new property in the *colonia*. First angered by news of the rent increase, Papi eventually took solace in knowing the family had been preparing for the transition. We began the transition by buying a mobile home on credit, and we then worked with another family that had purchased an adjoining lot to dig the ditches to lay down the water pipes to access water from the local water district. There was an interdependent quality to our first 10 years in our new country. Our parents learned from Toñita, they built community with kids and neighbors, and we all learned that being there for each other was a better way to live, and a better way to be good neighbors.

Contrary to the prevailing narrative of poverty as a deficit in this country, we grew up in a space and place of privilege, love, and hope. The economic conditions were difficult, to be sure, but our parents modeled how these social conditions were not determinants to what their children could become. They modeled how hard work and how the need for community were needed to change these conditions. Their work as community builders gave us an insight into how to do the work with a sense of gratitude. We learned about the importance of weaving a social fabric within the *barrio*. We learned about the availability of clothing closets at the local Sacred Heart Catholic church. We learned about free lunch at the school, about where we could take a shower and maintain good hygiene when we did not have running water or warm water during the winters during our first years in the *colonia*. Our training ground for life was defined by these conditions and by learning from our parents, and others such as Toñita Rodríguez, how to develop our own agency.

Moving from federal housing to a home with no potable running water, with no paved roads, nor the necessary heating to warm the home during the winter became a place for tense learning. We helped our father secure running water; we helped him seek electricity from the local power company; and we stood by as he lobbied the county commissioner to pave the road in our *colonia*. When the old mobile home we moved with us to the *colonia* began to fall apart, we built our own house, with our own hands, one cinder block at a time. We built the house in strategic steps as we secured the materials, the resources, and then enlisted assistance from local talent such as roofers and plumbers to lend a helping hand, even if they were fairly compensated. These community-building experiences in the

Figure 3. José Angel and Julia Guajardo 2005.

barrio guide how we build community in the classroom, in our communities, and through our research enterprise. We attempt to do this with the dignity, respect, humor, and gratitude that our father and mother taught us. The day our father passed, he died in the house we built, and his four sons (three PhDs among us, and all four with university degrees) standing by our mother, in love, in community, and in solidarity. We learned all this from our two most important mentors: *Papi y Mami* (see Figure 3).

Threats and the issue of race

Papi lived by the rule of responsibility to his family and to his community. His love of learning, his curiosity, and the constant change in life created the necessary tension for his own growth. Day-to-day activity in our living room, at the local coffee shop, or at the post office was the classroom experience that was part of his *Universidad de la Vida*. His curriculum was his lived experience, which he shared generously with everyone, primarily through his frequent *pláticas*. These experiences were not always noble or safe; he shared stories of hardship, stories of grief, and stories of tension that we would eventually face in public schools, as academics, or simply in life. He shared the story of the flight from Mexico because of a threat to his life. The story goes that when he was a *canalero* and was charged with dispensing water to farmers, a large landowner threatened to kill him if Papi did not allot the farmer more water for his fields. Papi refused to apportion more water, and rather than risk his life, he and Mami transplanted the family. Years later, he intimated that he could not imagine his young wife raising three small children by herself. Their instinct to leave the homeland and extended family was one of survivals. They had to trust that the alternative would be more sustainable in the long run, though not necessarily easier. It was a dramatic move, but our parents' actions tended toward the dramatic, in some cases even poetic. We came from Mexico the last day of 1968, the year historians claim changed the world – it was indeed the year that changed our lives. Every year, at the end of the year, Papi retold the story of the family migration. Each time he told it, he suggested it was a revolutionary act, moving from relative comfort, albeit in humble and low economic conditions, to a place of wild uncertainty. He made it seem biblical, as if something out of *Exodus*. Papi was given to hyperbole; it was part of his pedagogy. The power of the story was clear, and the powerful nature of storytelling became a central part of our own pedagogical approach (Behar, 1996; Delgado, 1989).

Even with the separation from our mother country and introduction to the United States, it was always clear to us that we were Mexicanos. We communicated in the language of Mexicanos. The aroma, the colors, the décor, and everything about our home mused the Mexican senses. Our home culture became our oxygen. Our parents continually reinforced the cultural traditions in proud ways, so we became proud ourselves. Issues of race and class were also part of home conversations, though Papi was always careful to share with us only lessons we were ready for – timing was important to him. One day we shared a story from school over the dinner table about use of language and racial identity that was the focus of a classroom discussion. Our experiences as migrant farm workers had exposed us to different racial dynamics in other parts of the country, and we had been able to compare racial treatment in South Texas to treatment in other places. When the school story came up, Papi felt it was the right time to share a troubling encounter he had experienced just a year before.

He first set the context by describing the farm where he worked, the Anglo *patrón*, his Mexicano co-workers, the workload, and equity in pay. He said that he earned $1 per hour while others earned significantly more than he did, even though he believed he worked harder and longer hours than the others. We recalled the time he worked 100 h in a week managing the irrigation of a field, and brought home $100 in wages. Nobody could question Papi's work ethic, but he felt he was in an exploitative circumstance. He said that after he and Mami had a series of *pláticas* about this issue, he found the courage to ask the Anglo farmer about his wages. As Papi told the story, he noted the Anglo farmer's prominent place in community life. The family had come to the area early in the twentieth century and had played a role in founding the town site. The family had a long established dairy farm, where Papi was employed during the time of this story. The day he approached the Anglo farmer with the question on wages, the farmer seemed annoyed. 'What is it you want to talk to me about,' the farmer said in Spanish – the Anglo farmer was fluently bilingual. Papi asked the farmer if he would consider paying a fairer wage. The farmer snickered, then responded:

> Guajardo, what gives you the right to ask me this question? Do you know that if I wanted to, I could kill you and throw you in the canal? The sad thing is that nobody would care, but your family.

With that, the conversation ended, abruptly.

An endearing quality of Papi's was that he thought people were mostly good, and if they said something cruel, they likely did not mean any harm. He asked the *patrón* a question to know if it were possible to make a little more money for his hard work. The threat ended the conversation, but this time he and Mami weren't leaving. They were in their new community to stay, and they stayed forever. Papi knew he had to be careful *con el gringo*, and he understood that he had to take the high road during tense and contentious times. He felt he could not challenge the white farmer fully, at least not in directly overt ways. Papi's resistance was different, and he exercised it by proving to the *gringo* that there was value in his life, and in the life of his family. In the ensuing decades, Papi and the farmer saw each other frequently, at the post office, the grocery store, and even drank coffee together at the local coffee shop and reminisced about old times. Papi used to say that in their old age, the *old gringo* came to appreciate him for the hard work he had done, and likely for the aggressions he endured. The *gringo* came to value the relationship enough that he sat for an oral history where our father himself conducted the interview. On this occasion, Papi was a lead researcher for a team of graduate students from our respective universities engaged in an oral history project on the Bracero Program. Papi filled the role the grad students could not, as he knew where the elders (the *braceros* and the farmers) were and knew how to get them to the interview. The old *gringo* had contracted many *braceros* between the 1940s and the early 1960s, and Papi sought him out and arranged to interview him. The interview was a thing of beauty, even if Papi could not get the *gringo* to accept that race relations were a critical issue in the history of the community. Posthumously, Papi became co-author in an article we wrote (Guajardo et al., 2014) on that oral history project on the Bracero Program. In the end, a profound expression of his resistance is that he authored his story and helped others tell theirs, including the *gringo's*, and in a peer-reviewed journal.

Papi modeled effective and relevant pedagogies throughout his life. He helped us develop our research, informed our teaching, and politicized our service. The politic we choose to practice is a behavior of engagement, one that is for the public good and in the interest of those who have little access to power. This also guides the way we negotiate our positions in the academy. We know what the powers and gatekeepers within the institution are capable of, and we respond to these challenges in a dignified and affirming way. Our father's experience with threats and the vulnerability they created is instructive. As much as academia is a place of great privilege, it is similarly a place rife with threats. Scholars of color particularly experience repeated micro-aggressions in their day-to-day life, a reality we have been privy to on countless occasions. Papi and Mami taught us how to deal with these aggressions, and they taught us the importance of healing … when people are ready. We have been rejected for promotion at one time or another, but we know that whatever our experience is, it is nowhere as challenging as the one Papi and Mami faced as young parents raising a family. We find hope, love, and healing in Papi's stories, as challenging and painful as they may be. Our parents even introduced us to micro-aggressions well before they were common in the literature. Their stories give direction to our work and give us permission to dream, and to be hopeful.

Curioso y preguntón

Mami has been the best mentor in dealing with people. Her influence touches everything we do in life, especially in our work as university professors. The 'go-to' question that often guides decision-making, particularly during times that require mediation, is 'what would Mami do?' Her ubiquitous presence gives clarity to our work, and to life. The other two mentors most consequential in showing us how to navigate academic life were Papi, and Enrique 'Henry' Trueba. Our father had a fourth-grade education in rural Mexico, but the *Universidad de la Vida* he attended provided the global experience he parlayed as mentor. Trueba came into our lives when we were in the doctoral program at the University of Texas in the late 1990s. He arrived in Austin with a distinguished record in education anthropology and educational leadership. A former Mexican Jesuit Priest, Trueba entered higher education in the United States in the mid 1960s. His academic stops included tenures as Dean at the University of Wisconsin, Provost at the University of Houston, and he was a member of the National Academy of Education. When he arrived in Austin in the late 1990s, he was in search of spiritual and emotional grounding, a place he could point to as the community of practice where he once said, 'That's how education for Latino children should be happening.' He found it, he said to us, when he began to read of our work with Llano Grande. At first, he believed Llano Grande was a mythical place, where rural Mexican American students who fit the profile as mostly low income, or immigrants or farm workers, were being prepared to attend the most competitive universities, many of them Ivy League schools, and a number of the students were graduating and coming back home to rural South Texas. We wrote about this narrative born out of Edcouch-Elsa High School and through the leadership of the Llano Grande Center for Research and Development, an organization we had founded (Guajardo & Guajardo, 2002, 2004, 2008; Guajardo, Guajardo, & Casaperalta, 2008; Guajardo, Guajardo, Janson, & Militello, 2016).

'I love this mythical place you guys call Llano Grande,' Trueba commented on one of our papers. When we convinced him the place was real, he told us he had to see it with his own eyes. So we brought Henry to South Texas, and after two days *in situ*, he called his wife Ardie to tell her they were leaving Austin, he was retiring from UT, and they were moving to the small town of Elsa, the physical home of the Llano Grande Center. Trueba bought an old historic home that sat on five acres, just north of Elsa, and quickly befriended our father. Papi had just retired as an elementary school janitor and along with building a close friendship with Trueba, he also took a job as his groundskeeper. But keeping the grounds was only the second responsibility he kept. Early in their relationship it became apparent that Trueba needed Papi more for the cultural and social energy he gave him, and Papi needed Trueba to get us through our PhD programs. They understood each other in those ways, but the deeper level of understanding vis-à-vis the cultural and emotional energy they provided each other was special. They appreciated each other's curious nature. Papi looked forward to Trueba's daily questions, and Trueba used to say that our father was *curioso y preguntón*, which translates into funny and curious (*curioso* as amusing). Trueba loved that Papi resembled himself as a curious ethnographer, which was how Trueba saw our father. He said our father was the only person he knew who asked more questions than he. Trueba saw Papi as a homegrown anthropologist, and he fed Papi by responding to his every question.

Trueba found Papi to be especially funny. The daily ritual was when he walked out of his house to call out: *Señor Guajardo, pase a tomar café, y a contarme un chiste or dos.* (Mr. Guajardo, come inside for a cup of coffee, and to share a joke or two.) Papi was happy to oblige, and he was always 'ready.' That was one of the truths about Papi, he was always 'ready,' *y siempre presente*. Trueba appreciated that Papi was always in the moment, and always ready to offer a story, or *anécdota*, to connect to whatever conversation. Trueba most loved Papi's humor, and he would laugh heartily. Trueba loved to laugh, and Papi's wide repertoire of Mexican *chistes* provoked Trueba's laughter, and fueled his anthropological sensibilities. When Trueba died in 2004, after a lengthy battle with cancer, he had just published his last book, *The New Americans*. He wrote the entire book at his new home in Elsa, and in between *chiste* sessions with our father. In his opening credits, Trueba honored Papi by calling him 'an organic intellectual,' and told the publisher to include a picture of Papi on the back cover. From cover-to-cover the celebrated anthropologist and his friend who was *curioso y preguntón* became part of the same book.

Henry Trueba theorized about pedagogy of hope and about organic intellectuals, and he found both in our father. In the South Texas space they shared together, Trueba came to see our father as more than a subject for an ethnographic study. He wrote about others he came across in the region, but with our father he kept the relationship more personal, as they found kinship in their life experiences as Mexicanos who had come to the United States. They were close in age, so that helped. They connected through sharing stories and memories of the homeland, even if the differences between the two were stark in terms of educational attainment and professional achievement. Trueba authored more than a dozen books, and was distinguished in his field. But he found a kindred soul in our father, because they cared about the same things. They cared about family, community, learning, and they loved to laugh. During the final years of his life, Trueba finally saw his theories come to life.

Trueba jokingly complained about Papi's inquisitive nature, but from the other side of his mouth, he praised it. He also joked that this same curiosity was the source of his own humor, and even scholarship. That same trait helps us understand the balance between intellect, relevance, humor, and respect. We didn't have this awareness as kids. We learned it later in life as we pursued our graduate studies, though humor and play as cornerstones of effective learning theory were dynamics we saw while growing up. We saw it in full display through the interactions of our father and Trueba. A lasting legacy left by our father is that as much as we may think our academic work is important, if we do not have fun with it, it probably is not worth what we think it is. Our father taught us that humor is as much personality as it is the product of investing in relationships. It is easier to have fun with those who trust you, and it is important to laugh with everyone. Trueba and Papi used to have extemporaneous laugh sessions, where their laughter begat more laughter. Those rich experiences also teach us that humor is important as we help others build their own agency and resilience during difficult social, cultural, and economic times.

The power of question is the act of curiosity. Papi taught us this skill through his behavior, and it became an effective tool that we use to teach, research, lead, and guide change processes. Trueba nurtured this in a higher education environment. We saw the praxis of curiosity and humor when our two mentors joined forces. In August 2002, one of us (Miguel) defended his dissertation at the University of Texas-Austin. Our parents and friends traveled for the event – Trueba joined us from his home in Houston. He was weak as he underwent treatment for prostate cancer. Still, he participated fully. A profound moment transpired in the middle of the formal defense, when Trueba called 'timeout' and began to explain to our parents what was happening. As monolingual Spanish speakers, our parents did not understand most of the presentation, which was delivered in English. But Trueba sensed the curiosity in our parents, and in an act of great respect, he stopped the proceeding and translated the defense into Spanish. At that point, everyone was able to share in the learning process, an important lesson we employ with our students when they defend. It is important that everyone be aware what is taking place, especially parents and grandparents who attend dissertation defenses and who may not understand the language.

Upon completion of the defense, and as we left the classroom, Trueba leaned to Papi and said, *Señor Guajardo, ahora sigue Paco*! (Mr. Guajardo, now Paco is next [to defend his dissertation].) One year later, Francisco defended his dissertation in the same classroom and through the same Trueba-led translated process. For the first time in his academic career, Trueba brought his wife Ardie to a dissertation defense. It was the last defense Trueba would attend, as he would pass on months later. He was prophetic in his work, as he told our father after the last dissertation defense, *Señor Guajardo, ya cumplimos. Sus dos hijos se graduaron. Ya puedo morir en paz.* (Mr. Guajardo, we have fulfilled our goal, both your sons have graduated. I can now die in peace.)

Learning from dying, a theory of change

Through the life and death of our father, we glean key components of a theory of change and action. The model he presented through the years demonstrates how relationships, assets, stories, place, politic, and action come together. The vitality of relationships comes from every story; it can be taken amply from the value Papi held toward his relationship with Polo. The assets are found in the personal qualities of being *cumplido*, of framing life experience as rich curriculum, of the books he kept from grade school, of understanding that he and his family held high value. The parables in his stories serve as deep lessons for how to live, how to teach, how to learn. He appreciated his village in rural Mexico

Figure 4. José Ángel hovers over grave of his brother, Pedro Guajardo, 1995.

because he reflected on how it had shaped his sense of self, and he found value in the place, just as we have found our place where we were raised as a treasure land. He behaved in honest ways, and lived a life of integrity as he practiced a politic for the public good. And he acted on things, with or without others, though he mostly understood that with others he could accomplish far more.

Papi modeled a life of integrity as a public citizen. It is why our work bends toward academic activism. The lessons he taught us as children inspire how we practice our research, how we teach our classes, and how we engage in service. We do community work because it strengthens our spirit, informs our research, and guides our teaching. The work is interwoven into the three strands, and manifests itself as a hybrid brand of research in action that allows us to work at the university, in public schools, and in communities. We give back, just like our father did. Being a public person is about helping out, about *ayudando al próxima* (helping your neighbor) – a lesson our father learned from his mother. The wisdom from his mother, our *Abuela* Virginia, echoes in much of what we do, as they laid out the model for reciprocity in a simple axiom: *ayer fuí yo, hoy son mis vecinos, y mañana son mis hijos* (yesterday it was me, today it is our neighbors, and tomorrow it will be my children).

For Papi, working for the public good began with his children. He gave to others because at some point in life his children would need a hand. We struggle with the currency and the values of academia, but we find strength in knowing the work we do is based on working for the public good. We will negotiate the priorities of the institution, because our academic positions and training dictate we do so, but helping communities grow stronger and sustainable is at the heart of the work. We are committed to living a life of tensions where we face challenges, but we also celebrate victories, special occasions, and cultural experiences, like we did the last day of our father's life. He also had a dramatic quality in his personality, and in the way he lived life. He was a master storyteller, an effective community builder, and a public performer. He died on the same day he turned 77, on the 19 May 2013. The day his family said goodbye was the same day we sang happy birthday and ate cake. It was a day to celebrate a life, a legacy, and a spirit that lives in the teaching, service, and research we practice. Papi's way was revolutionary and transformational. We only attempt to be like him (Figure 4).

Disclosure statement

No potential conflict of interest was reported by the authors.

References

Ah Nee-Benham, M. K. P. (1998). *Culture and educational policy in Hawai'i: The silencing of native voices*. Mahwah, NJ: L. Erlbaum Associates.

Ah Nee-Benham, M. K. P., & Cooper, J. E. (Eds.). (2000). *Indigenous educational models for contemporary practice: In our mother's voice*. Mahwah, NJ: L. Erlbaum Associates.

Anzaldúa, G. (1987). *Borderlands – La Frontera: The New Mestiza*. San Francisco, CA: Aunt Lute Press.

Behar, R. (1996). *The vulnerable observer: Anthropology that breaks your heart*. Boston, MA: Beacon Press.

Delgado, R. (1989). Storytelling for oppositionists and others: A plea for narrative. *Michigan Law Review, 87*, 411–441.

Delgado-Bernal, D., Elenes, C. A., Godinez, F. E., & Villenas, S. (Eds.). (2006). *Chicana/Latina education in everyday life: Feminista perspectives on pedagogy and epistemology*. Albany, NY: State University of New York Press.

Freire, P. (1998). *Pedagogy of freedom: Ethics, democracy, and civic courage*. New York, NY: Rowman and Littlefield.

Freire, P. (2000). *Pedagogy of the oppressed* (30th anniv. ed.). New York, NY: Continuum.

Freire, P. (2002). *Pedagogy of hope*. New York, NY: Continuum. (Original work published 1992)

González, N., Moll, L. C., & Amanti, C. (Eds.). (2005). *Funds of knowledge: Theorizing practice in households, communities, and classrooms*. Mahwah, NJ: Erlbaum Associates.

Guajardo, J. A. (1988). *Ancedotas de mi vida*. Unpublished autobiography of José Ángel Guajardo. Elsa, TX.

Guajardo, F., Alvarez, S., Guajardo, M., Garcia, S., Guajardo, J. A., & Marquez, J. (2014). Braceros, Mexicans, American, and Schools: Re-imagining teaching and learning in Mexican America. *Rio Bravo Journal, 23*, 9–41.

Guajardo, M., & Guajardo, F. (2002). Critical ethnography and community change. In H. Trueba, & Y. Zou (Eds.), *Ethnography and schools: Qualitative approaches to the study of education* (pp. 281–304). Lanham, MD: Rowman & Littlefield.

Guajardo, M., & Guajardo, F. (2004). The impact of Brown on the Brown of South Texas: A micropolitical perspective on the education of Mexican Americans in a small rural community. *American Educational Research Journal, 41*, 501–526.

Guajardo, M., & Guajardo, F. (2008). Two brothers in higher education: Weaving a social fabric for service in academia. In K. P. González & R. V. Padilla (Eds.), *Doing the public good: Latina/o scholars engage civic participation* (pp. 74–98). Sterling, VA: Stylus Publications.

Guajardo, M., Guajardo, F., & Casaperalta, E. (2008). Transformative education: Chronicling a pedagogy for social change. *Anthropology & Education Quarterly, 39*, 3–22.

Guajardo, M., Guajardo, F., Janson, C. & Militello, M. (2016). *Reframing community partnerships in education: Uniting the power of place and wisdom of people*. New York, NY: Routledge.

Patton, M. Q. (2002). *Qualitative research & evaluation methods*. Thousand Oaks, CA: Sage.

Reyes, P., Scribner, J. D., & Paredes-Scribner, A. (1999). *Lessons from high performing Hispanic school: Creating learning communities*. New York, NY: Teachers College Press.

Scheurich, J. J., & Young, M. D. (1997). Coloring epistemologies: Are our research epistemologies racially biased? *Educational Researcher, 26*, 4–16.

Trueba, E. T. (1999). *Latinos unidos: From cultural diversity to the politics of solidarity*. Lanham, MD: Rowman & Littlefield.

Trueba, E. T. (2004). *The new Americans: Immigrants and transnationals at work*. Lanham, MD: Rowman & Littlefield Publishers.

Valenzuela, A. (1999). *Subtractive schooling: U.S.-Mexican youth and the politics of caring*. Albany, NY: State University of New York Press.

Vygotsky, L. S. (1978). *Mind in society: The development of higher psychological processes*. Cambridge, MA: Harvard University Press.

Breaking into public policy circles for the benefit of underserved communities

Stella M. Flores

ABSTRACT

Stella M. Flores writes about how she learned to participate in the American political process through lessons from her immigrant family. As a quantitative scholar, she documents the commitment to rigorous, evidence-based research on equity noting that not all datasets are without politics or bias. From this perspective, the story of the Latino in the US has only recently begun to be collected. The author describes her development as a female scholar of color in the field of education policy, an identity informed by her experiences growing up in South Texas. She credits role models, mentors, and generational impact from educational opportunity as key reasons for engaging in scholarship aimed to help improve educational attainment rates for underserved students. She argues that regardless of methodological tradition, scholars working toward improving the educational trajectories for all students are in many ways activists for the common good and not necessarily unobtrusive analysts.

'Uvas no!' 'Huelga! Huelga!' When I was about six years old, my grandmother told me to chant these words. I did what I was told, though I had no idea what I was saying. It was the early 1980s, and I recall being in a crowded room in South Texas, where an Austin Democratic politician was visiting a group of United Farm Workers in the Rio Grande Valley. It was hot, and I was too short to see anything but the bottoms and backs of everyone around me, but I still remember the energy in that room – it was strong, passionate, urgent, and hopeful.

About 17 years later my grandmother and I were again at another political rally in South Texas, this time in the outdoor beastly heat. The crowd was enthusiastically cheering 'Cleentón! Cleentón!' as President Bill Clinton was introduced by local radio and television legend Johnny Canales. I was still shorter than most in the crowd, although this time, I could at least see the stage. I was absolutely miserable standing in the heat, but I felt that if my aged grandmother expressed no discontent, then I had better not complain. Our grandmother, whom we called *Mama Lola*, was tougher than nails, and she had made her peace with the sun many years prior to this event, when she worked in the fields of the farmlands across the nation.

Participating in the American political process was essential in my family, and these experiences shaped my own development as a policy scholar and represent how many immigrant voters and their families begin to understand public policy. No matter how irrelevant these chants may be to those walking the hallways in Washington, my grandmother's faithful support of her candidates meant the world to her, and she wanted her children and grandchildren to know how moments like that could help to change the system for the poor and disenfranchised.

Mama Lola cherished her adopted country and had faith that living here would continue to improve the quality of life her children and grandchildren would experience. By the time of that Clinton rally, we had nearly lost my mother to cancer – ultimately a critical and profound loss – but my grandmother remained engaged in politics and hopeful about the American dream. Today, when I'm working in my New York City office, staring at a screen full of census numbers, I often think of the immigrant grand-mothers and their citizen grandchildren represented in the data. And I remember the five-year old girl, my mother, who was brought into this country on the shoulders of her father as they crossed the Rio Grande. It was not her decision to leave Mexico or even her father's – it was my grandmother who made the decision, taking great risks so she would have a chance to provide a better life for her family, then and for generations to come. My grandmother, who had only a third-grade education, gave me the gift of believing that our family's story is part of the American fabric and I have a place in making American public policy. This is the ideal that has fueled my work, and my world.

I am a scholar of American public policy in the areas of education and immigration. I consider myself a social scientist, and most of my work is in the quantitative tradition. I believe in asking probing ques-tions and designing studies that will help to reduce bias, my aim being to get a clearer picture of what causes inequality so we can determine what interventions may reduce inequality and give underrep-resented students better odds of educational attainment. I also spend considerable time chasing data to construct these studies and evaluating current work in the field. While so doing, I have discovered that data and the processes that surround their collection and production are not free of either politics or bias. For example, 'Hispanics' were not considered an official group in the US Census until nearly the 1970s, although Latinos had begun to establish their place in history well before the founding of the United States (Cohn, 2010; San Miguel, 2004).

The Latino story has only recently begun to be documented in comparison to other groups, and our understanding of our strengths, challenges, and potential are not yet fully captured in any data-sets. However, this does not deter me from producing strongly designed quantitative research. My experiences as a Latina from South Texas who graduated from Harvard and was tenured at Vanderbilt University have shown me that few spaces are free of either bias or privilege. In the stories that follow, I will share how my experiences have shaped my vision of public policy, which can be helpful in acknowl-edging inequality and designing new structures to promote educational equity, and in challenging ourselves to support not only our own communities but others that are fighting for educational equity in the United States and beyond.

As a researcher, the roles self-reflection and context play in writing about underrepresented com-munities are of particular importance. In my interactions with other quantitative education scholars around the country, I find that many of us bring critical personal stories into our work. White, Latino, Black, immigrant, Asian, poor, low-income, first-generation college goers, women – all of our identities influence how we define and tackle a problem.

At the time I write this, given the circles in which I have chosen to share my work and energy, I recognize that I made an agreement with myself to be a person who unapologetically supports the promotion of educational opportunity, advancement for underserved communities, and the reduc-tion of inequality. I do not support the policies of hate or exclusion that are now so common in many state legislatures, but I realize that we do not always know what method or policy will produce the most positive outcomes for underserved communities. I therefore support the collection of evidence to construct strong study designs that will help provide answers to these important questions, which can be approached both from a qualitative and quantitative perspective. One thing already evident is that many educational policies are exclusionary or created with bad intentions. However, the research is quite strong (Hout, 2012; Moretti, 2004) that investments in education produce private and social returns to both individuals and their communities (Moretti, 2004), in particular individuals who other-wise are not likely to pursue postsecondary education (Hout, 2012).

Figure 1. My mother, grandmother, and aunt on a tourist break during a migrant farmworkers' trip in the Midwest in 1970. My mother was a college student at this time.

The following stories provide a portrait of my development as an educational policy researcher. Hard working does not begin to describe the family I have the privilege to be part of. My paternal grandmother was a school custodian and my maternal grandmother was a farmworker who worked in the fields throughout her pregnancies. I am the daughter of farmworkers-turned college graduates. My paternal grandfather served in World War II as a soldier and cook and my maternal grandfather was a *bracero,* a farmworker hired through the 1940s guest-worker program. My father began working at the age of nine, collecting trash at a drive-in theater. My mother worked as a caretaker and a housekeeper during college. I am the first of this generation to not have to work in the fields as a farmworker. As a result, I am the family member of my generation who has the responsibility to document how investments in education, financial aid, and workforce policy can make a difference for future generations of the poor in the United States (Figure 1).

My family has always played an important role in my motivation to enter the field of education. However, the person who most powerfully guides my role as a researcher is my mother, a former teacher. My mother was part of what is referred to as the 1.5-generation student, a foreign-born student who attends high school in the US (Crosnoe & Turley, 2011). She was the cultural, gender, and educational intermediary in my development, for a number of reasons. Although I grew up in a supportive family environment, I was still a girl/woman in South Texas. My mother mediated gender roles, standing up to my grandmother and father on decisions that she knew would lead to greater opportunity for me – going away to college, studying abroad – and with her philosophy on my choosing whom to marry, or whether to marry at all. She taught me about my responsibility to change the world, to help others who were less advantaged than I. She also told me, in no uncertain terms, 'Of course you can get a PhD by the time you are 30!' I didn't quite meet her goal, as I was 32 when I received my doctoral degree from Harvard, but her spirit was and still is with me every day, and the goals she set for me still motivate me today, even though she passed away from cancer when I was 22. As I write this, I know that I am not done striving to reach these goals, and that our story of mother and daughter is not yet complete.

An introduction to the history of race relations in the US

While my grandmother cemented in us the value of political participation, my mother's contribution was no less important. She had an understanding of US race relations and gender roles that went far beyond what one might expect of a woman living in a town that was nearly 90% Hispanic and 10% White. My mother used television and movies to illustrate the history of another disenfranchised group, African-Americans. I remember a radical shift in our television viewing, from the latest *telenovela* on Spanish television to Alex Hailey's *Roots*. Shortly thereafter, I saw and then read Alice Walker's *The Color Purple*. I didn't understand it all, but I knew these were stories of survival, pain, injustice, sacrifice and triumph. Decades later, upon watching the musical, *The Color Purple*, on Broadway, the message became extraordinarily clear: Fight for others, but also for yourself.

I remember one particular conversation between my mother and my father, which I was not supposed to hear. She told him she would support whomever I chose to marry, regardless of race. I don't know how the conversation started (my hypothesis is that it was when I asked for a Michael Jackson doll for Christmas), but her message was clear – all people deserve justice, compassion, and love, and there should be no boundaries between people because of skin color. Through reading and other media, I knew more about the Black experience than my own community; that knowledge would come later, in my college sociology and Chicano literature courses. Television had shown me that I could go away to college, study abroad, and maybe even attend an Ivy League institution. I based my own dreams on these television representations of young black women attending college in the 1990s.

But then there was Sheila E, the Latina drummer. Sheila E introduced me to an impossible idea – to be part of the gender-biased world of drumming. If my parents blinked, I didn't see it. They fully supported their 11-year-old Mexican American daughter's outrageous request to play the drums in the school band. Like my grandmother's unwavering belief that we had a right to the American political process, my parents gave me their unwavering support to develop this talent. And thus I became a drummer. This experience was the best training I could have for later tests of my persistence. I faced battles of gender, race, and height discrimination, which provided lessons that would serve me long after I left high school. Learning discipline, persistence, and the goal to be the best in one's field were all part of this experience.

Continued encounters with civil rights issues

My first personal encounter with civil rights occurred in a fifth-grade middle school classroom. The students were all in a buzz about what activity they would choose in the sixth grade: choir, orchestra, or band. I had definitely decided on band, and I wanted to play something strong that would give me a presence. My classmate Joe said he was going to play the drums. I said enthusiastically, 'I'm going to play the drums, too!' to which Joe replied, 'Girls don't play the drums, Stella.' Joe would remain a thorn in my side until senior year, which helped to make me a stronger drummer. We competed against each other constantly, but deep down I felt he respected me. Joe had a natural talent for drumming, and though I beat him more often than he beat me, I really had to work at it. Years later, while I was attending a conference in graduate school, I ran into Joe at a hotel where he was working. Our lives had changed dramatically, but there was still fondness. I had always had a soft spot for him, as his easy talent had made me envious and motivated me to work harder. Eventually, I became one of the first female drummers for the school's jazz band, and we received top marks at state competitions. I would be remiss if I didn't also mention my drum teacher, a man who offered the kind of tough love that made you know you would not get anything for free. His philosophy was that you get it if you earn it. This created an atmosphere that made me eager to compete with all I had, especially against anyone who thought I didn't deserve a spot in the band because of my size or gender.

My experience in the drum corps made me realize that my differences made people uncomfortable. This was a new for me because nearly 90% of my high school was Hispanic, and I had not felt the stigma of difference until I joined the drum line. It was an adjustment for the boys, and their discomfort was sometimes obvious from their attitude and comments. This experience has been all too familiar and persistent to me as a woman of color in academia and the policy world: *my presence disrupts the status quo*. I sometimes ask myself why I claim these spaces and why I persist, and I think the answer is that my mother and grandmother gave me the gift of daring to believe I belong in these spaces and that I have a right to claim the rights afforded me.

While choosing to play the drums started off as a political statement, it also brought me indescribable pleasure and an interesting form of power in unpredictable places. I would use this skill while attending graduate school at Harvard, a time that was very stressful and lonely, as I was so far from my family. It was because of a conversation over Texas and music with some Chicano classmates from the school of education that we suddenly decided to form a band called *Frontera* Rock. We were entertaining at best, but it was a form of cultural expression we needed for ourselves and for our small community of students of color in 'el norte.' I was by no means another Sheila E, but the experience of forming a Latino rock band that played Carlos Santana songs gave me fuel to survive the winter – and to write my qualifying paper so I could move on to the dissertation phase (Figure 2).

Figure 2. Performing at the Abbey in Cambridge, Massachusetts, October 2004.

The role of mentors

A former Mexican American professor from Texas once called some of us doctoral students 'well-adjusted border children.' I didn't get what he meant until I began to understand the role of mentors and racial representation in the academy. As noted, I grew up in South Texas in a town that was 90% Hispanic, which meant that two realties framed our upbringing: demographic power and lack of financial power. The demography of the border had evolved considerably since my parents were in school in the 1960s, when they still had to ride different buses than the white students. By the time I was coming of age as a high school student, the border area had a majority of Mexican-origin teachers, judges, lawyers, and political officials. Financial power, in the form of owning ranchlands or banks and other traditional measures of wealth, was not as well distributed across the population, but I nevertheless grew up having no doubt that I could be a lawyer, teacher, or even a political official. Being born to two college-educated parents had certainly given me the gift of confidence, but the demographic representation that surrounded me also played an important role. This became clear to me during my college experience in the 1990s, when I was first in environment where the cleaning staff was predominantly Latino and the cooking staff African-American. The students were mostly white, except for a small sample of students of color. There was only one Mexican American female professor on campus, and when I took her class my world was forever changed. My mother had told me numerous times that I could get my doctorate, but I didn't fully believe her until I met Dr. Angela Valenzuela.

Scholars have written extensively about the academic, social, and psychological effects of mentoring (Crisp & Cruz, 2009). Like the evolving demography of Texas, the landscape of effective mentorship is also constantly changing. My own approach to mentoring my students now is a product of how I engaged in and negotiated the mentorship experiences I have had since leaving South Texas. My mentoring began with a powerful Chicana sociology professor, continued during my master's program with Chicano and African-American professors, and evolved into having a community of caretakers, mostly other Latino professors who probably didn't know how critical they were to my persisting in my doctoral program at Harvard. They gave me what I knew as informal academic community mentoring, which consisted of giving me a place of refuge during my visits to Texas. These scholars took time out of their busy days to have lunch with me, invite me to their homes and their schools, and to listen as I told them about the challenges and opportunities I was finding along the way.

While most of my mentors were education scholars, our methodological approaches differed significantly, but all shared my goal of improving the education system for Latinos and other underrepresented students. Their mentorship and friendship continue to contribute to the sustainability of scholars of color, current and future, in academia. Their care and time helped to construct this policy scholar, which in turn has helped me guide my own students. At a time when there is great temptation to engage in methodological wars, stepping back to see the larger picture – including the value of mentoring our students so they can be the best teachers and researchers possible, regardless of their scholarly bent – seems much more productive, for them and for society. I always will be grateful to my Texas mentors and friends for stepping in at a time in my journey when my first mentor, my mother, was no longer around to push me to the next level of the academic career ladder. I note this because it is another form of activism in the academy – sustaining the spirit of those in the journey for equity in society and in the academy through mentorship and example. They did this with no expectation of personal return on that investment. I strive to follow this example.

By the time I finished my graduate work at Harvard, I understood the value of mentorship and knew to look for it in various places. At Harvard, I was trained by a White civil rights scholar and a Black economist, and also supported by a number of White mentors who at times believed in me more than I did in myself. In one case, when I had reached a significant crossroad in my academic preparation, a White female mentor organized an intervention to convince me to take a series of quantitative courses that would begin to define my identity as a scholar. I remember feeling tired and isolated in my courses and didn't want to be the 'only one' again in the statistics sequence. The teachers and friends this mentor brought together pushed me to take the next step, which I no longer thought I had in me at the time.

This multiracial coalition of caretakers – my mentors, friends, and teachers – are responsible for a critical part of my development as a scholar. I am forever grateful for the tough love they used to usher me into my current career.

Reflections on traveling and researching abroad

Inequality is a persistent force across the world, and access to equitable educational opportunity is an equation no one country has mastered. My travels across the world have consistently illuminated this fact. I first traveled to Chile as a junior in college in the mid-1990s as part of a university study abroad program. We were led by an unassuming yet powerful Spanish American literature professor, Ricardo Yamal, who would pass away from a heart ailment soon after our return from Chile. Dr. Yamal was a native Chilean, and his return to his home country after many years of political strife was a meaningful event. The 1990s saw the 20th anniversary of the military coup against Salvador Allende's socialist government, which was led by Augusto Pinochet and his army. We were housed with middle-class Chilean families and attended what was considered an activist public university in Santiago. The dichotomy of this arrangement was striking but unspoken. At the time, I was not specifically focused on educational inequalities in particular. Instead, we listened to the stories of some children of the *desaparecidos;* some were told with many embellishments but most were not. I was fully bilingual, so I took this opportunity to learn from my new classmates, to explore and listen. While attending school in Chile, I did not participate in the ongoing demonstrations. I simply walked by or watched to try to understand more about the situation. I once got caught in a cloud of tear gas, one of the most physically painful experiences of my life but also one of the most important. While in Chile, I learned to understand myself and my values, and cemented a newfound independence and a love of studying other cultures. The experience ignited in me a desire to examine the trajectory of opportunity in another context. College access trajectories for the underserved are now a key part of my research.

Upon my return to the university, a Latino male student commented that I had come back from Chile 'so assertive and confident.' I happily responded with a 'thank you!' It was not until a few days later that I realized he did not mean this as a compliment. My continued interactions with this person exposed our conflicting perceptions about gender roles and stereotypes. This was something I had already confronted, so I moved around it and kept focused on my college goals and my future purpose.

While I was in Chile my mother's cancer was in remission, and her health was more stable than it had been over the previous two years. We both saw this as precious and valuable time for me to continue my college education, while she received care from the family at home in South Texas and got relief from the constant medical treatments at the cancer center in Houston. Her remission period gave me the confidence and sense of security to travel abroad for a semester. It was a difficult decision, but it was my mother's gift to me to go away without guilt.

Fourteen years after I first visited Chile, a former advisor recommended me for a panel on higher education access in Santiago, where low-income high schools in the area were trying out a version of the top 10 Percent plan with participating selective universities. The motivation for the program was that it would allow a certain percentage of high school seniors who completed a specific college access and preparation program to enter a selective college for free. The conference, which was held during the first year of the pilot program, consisted of academics talking about effective college access interventions in the US and France, along with students who were among the first to participate in the program.

I had been writing about the pros and cons of the Texas Top 10 Percent Plan relative to the consideration of race as a factor in college admissions. At the conference I presented my work on this topic and offered recommendations for the Chilean program. While analyses of the percent plan in the US proved it to be less successful than the use of affirmative action in college admissions, it was not yet clear whether the strategy proposed in Chile could be more successful than that used in Texas, particularly since the two contexts were so different.

The conversations were fascinating and useful in preparing future research. However, what I remember most about this conference is not those scholarly conversations but my conversations with the newly enrolled college students who were part of the program. They had been relatively quiet during the conference but were quite talkative at the luncheon. One student told me they had been listening to me and then said, *'Tu eres como nosotros, tu nos entiendes, verdad?'* ('You are like us, you understand us, right?') These students could see the symbols of my class background much better than anyone I had known in the US. No number of degrees can hide where you come from, nor should they. I learned that day that my message and my research hold a different power than I had thought. While I had come to Chile to share rigorous research, I left feeling like a symbol of what opportunity could do for the underserved. I didn't suffer the poverty they experience every day, yet the story of these students in Chile was that of my parents. I represented the next generational outcome of their struggle and success. I still carry their sacrifice and motivation with me in more ways than I knew possible.

Teaching in the 'Old South'

My most recent adventure was teaching in the American South at a selective private university. This experience was the greatest learning curve of my life to date, as I had never before experienced such a combination of contextual, demographic, and historical changes. For one thing, the Texas I know is not considered the deep South and it has a relationship, however rocky, with Latinos, and there is a degree of familiarity among the people of multiple races and national origins. At Harvard, I studied the effects of the civil rights movement in the South and had wondered what it would be like to be an activist during that period. After my first year in Tennessee, however, I didn't want any part in the struggle in that part of the country. In my first year, there I experienced enough harassment in the stores and in the voting booth to consider the move a mistake, despite the opportunity my university offered me for academic and research advancement. At the time it was the height of the anti-immigrant movement in the state, and every other political television commercial featured a crowd of angry Mexicans climbing the border walls. Latinos were unfamiliar in Tennessee and not at all understood. I had to assure even other Latinos in the area that I was an American citizen and that I could speak English.

Then, in 2009, Nashville took a stand. The mayor at the time, religious leaders, and businesses organized to defeat an English-only proposition in the city. By 2015, a bill to provide in-state resident tuition for undocumented immigrants failed to pass by only one vote – progress that was unimaginable in 2007. I had come to Tennessee as an expert on the effect in-state resident tuition policies had on undocumented student enrollment. My role as a scholar was to inform community activists, legislators, and families about the research, and recommend how to translate these results and the work of others into public policy. While I have advised national groups and other states on similar matters, my policy training told me this in-state tuition policy had a very low likelihood of passing in this part of the country. But likelihood is not necessarily destiny, and the outcome, a loss by one vote, showed there was indeed light at the end of the tunnel.

I left Tennessee for New York with some renewed hope for the future that at one time I had been too discouraged to muster up. The battle for educational opportunity in the South is different from that in other states. Tennessee was a new case for me in terms of legislative behavior on state policies. But it is also an area with old and new forms of community and cultural wealth, given its place in history as a location with no long-term Latino presence and a currently expanding Latino demographic. Other states in the South are facing similar circumstances, and the lessons to be learned from these communities are only beginning to be shared in the research literature.

Conclusion

I have often thought about being described as a 'well-adjusted border child' during my educational trajectory. I realize that, despite the lack of resources in towns along the border, the rich example I was raised with is truly invaluable. I now have a number of adult privileges – citizenship, secure finances, multiple degrees, mobility, tenure, and respect within my profession. While analysts call the Rio Grande Valley of Texas one of the 'third world' areas of the US, I remember it as a place of strength and critical support for what I have accomplished to date. As a Latina academic who studies public policy, I often reflect on my father's contribution to my policy career, and still hear his logical yet compassionate voice in my head. The lessons he imparted were informed by his own experiences as a low-income child and his profession as a social worker. He had a heart bigger than Texas along with a keen logic and instinct to analyze if, when, and how government could be of help to those in need. Although we didn't always agree on solutions, he always took the time to listen to my proposals with respect. When we discussed policy issues, he saw me an individual with credentials and not as a woman with too much ambition who didn't know her place. My father gave me voice among other men by allowing me to have a voice with him. He has since also passed away but he remains my policy to practice hero. His work was to help the disabled find jobs and go to college, and we saw him support his clients' courage and persistence beyond what any of us could have imagined. Visiting him at work throughout my childhood and seeing the gratitude and accomplishments expressed by many of his clients gave me enormous pride, but also put pressure on me to not give up on others – or on myself.

My continued concern is for the children who are growing up in areas without positive role models, and where the political messages they receive from their federal, state and local governments is that they are not worth any investment. No child should ever feel this kind of neglect or hatred. In such locations, the need is dire for legislators, educators, and caretakers who can counteract these negative messages through their actions, stories, encouragement, and documentation (Figure 3).

Figure 3. Flores with friends, family, and her prized piñata at her third birthday party in South Texas.

Ultimately, I define myself as an evidence-based scholar whose work is informed by principles of equity, access to opportunity, and strong research design. The mentors and teachers in my life, who both formally and informally call themselves activist scholars, are active in the pursuit for educational progress for all students in their own ways. The stories in this essay present a portrait of investment in an individual for the benefit of the larger community and, ultimately, the nation. This in itself is a form of activism for the common good. Producing strong and sustainable educators is a bold decision but also a very sensible way to improve society. In the end, I think true educators are more activists for the common good than unobtrusive analysts. Our methods may differ, but the commitment to produce research to improve the educational outcomes of the underserved is one we should make with pride. Some scholars call this investment in human capital, others may call it social justice, but whatever the term, educators can make few greater commitments than a long-term investment in a child's educational trajectory and well-being. I therefore end with the image I first introduced in this essay – the grandchild learning from her grandmother about the American system of politics, economics, and equal opportunity. This image reinforces the call for a multigenerational investment in the family as a way to promote the sustainability of a common good for all.

Disclosure statement

No potential conflict of interest was reported by the author.

References

Cohn, D. (2010). *Census history: Counting Hispanics.* Washington, DC: Pew Research Center. Retrieved February 2015, from http://www.pewsocialtrends.org/2010/03/03/census-history-counting-hispanics-2/

Crisp, G., & Cruz, I. (2009). Mentoring college students: A critical review of the literature between 1990 and 2007. *Research in Higher Education, 50,* 525–545. doi:10.1007/s11162-009-9130-2

Crosnoe, R., & Turley, R. N. (2011). K-12 educational outcomes of immigrant youth. *The Future of Children, 21,* 129–152.

Hout, M. (2012). Social and economic returns to college education in the United States. *Annual Review of Sociology, 38,* 379–400.

Moretti, E. (2004). Estimating the social return to higher education. *Journal of Economics, 121,* 175–212.

San Miguel, G. (2004). *Contested policy: The rise and fall of federal bilingual education in the United States, 1960–2001.* Dallas: University of North Texas Press.

Living the consciousness: navigating the academic pathway for our children and communities

Kaiwipunikauikawēkiu Lipe and Daniel 'Bubba' Lipe

ABSTRACT

This article chronicles how the authors, two Indigenous activist-academics, live into their consciousness, privileges, and responsibilities by realizing their roles through genealogical reflection. In particular, they focus on their responsibilities as change agents because of their reciprocal and interdependent roles as community members, as husband–wife partners, and as parents to their two children. Through the use of critical self-reflection, photography, and mo'olelo (a Native Hawaiian method of sharing inter-connected stories), the authors present a radically different and Indigenous approach to leadership, scholarship, and engagement that is rooted in genealogical connections to people, place, and knowledge systems. Though the authors experience tension as their Indigenous values rub up against those of the Western wvvorld of academia, their story exemplifies their resilience as the result of the love and commitment they have to their families and communities.

An introductory story: the work we do

Each Saturday morning, our family[1] piles into our gray Honda Civic and heads to town from the windward side of our island home of O'ahu. We drive over the mountain through the Likelike[2] Tunnel, across the city of Honolulu, until we finally arrive at the University of Hawai'i at Mānoa. There, awaiting our arrival is my (Kaiwipuni's) class of students.

In some ways, this story seems typical. We go to a university and I teach a class. What is unique, even precious however, is that my group of 'students' is comprised of mostly Native Hawaiian elders between the ages of 70 and 85 years old. Though raised in Hawai'i in Hawaiian households, many of them were physically punished for speaking Hawaiian language in their schools. This was a result of the 1896 law by the illegal white Provisional Government of Hawai'i[3] that sought to terminate Hawaiian language ('Aha Pūnana Leo, 2015; Benham & Heck, 1998) and all things Hawaiian (Kamins, 1998; Trask, 1992). Hence, my students were born into this era in which it was illegal to speak their mother tongue in school. It was not until 1978 that the Hawaiian language was finally recognized as an official language of the State of Hawai'i and in 1986 the Hawai'i State legislature allowed Hawaiian language to be a medium of instruction in public schools ('Aha Pūnana Leo, 2015). By the time this occurred, most of my students were well into their forties.

At the same time as being forced into Western assimilation through the public education system, my students were also deprived of their native tongue at home. Their parents, most of whom were native speakers of Hawaiian language, witnessed and experienced the racism associated with speaking

Hawaiian in a quickly Americanizing Hawai'i. Hence, they consciously withheld Hawaiian language from their children – my students – in the name of love and hope for a future they saw as inevitably American and English-centric.

Although between 1896 and 1986 Hawai'i and Native Hawaiians were forced into assimilation, steadfast keepers of Hawaiian language and culture persevered often in secret. Over the last 40 years, with the help of these Hawaiian practitioners, Hawai'i has experienced a Hawaiian renaissance. Interest and revitalization of Hawaiian language, culture, and knowledge systems has resulted and there is now an upswing of children and families speaking Hawaiian and drawing strength from their Hawaiian identity.[4]

My students, though recovering from the intergenerational trauma of oppression and colonization (Minton, personal communication, ongoing), have witnessed this renaissance and intentionally decided to join in. Today, in the last dozen or so years of their lives, they are fearlessly engaging in learning Hawaiian language, hula,[5] music, and chant; all birthrights they were stripped of during their youth (Maunakea-Forth, personal communication, April 25, 2013).

I, a 32-year old Hawaiian woman, a 'baby' compared to their seasoned experiences, am their Hawaiian language teacher. I am a product of the courageous and revolutionary commitment of a handful of the Hawaiian Language and Studies educators who began organizing in 1983 for the survival of Hawaiian language ('Aha Pūnana Leo, 2015). During this time period, my mother was writing her doctoral dissertation focused around the question: How did Hawaiians lose control of our land?[6] Her groundbreaking research and analysis catapulted her to become one of the leading Hawaiian historians of her time and has contributed greatly to the Hawaiian renaissance through education. Thus, when my mother made the intentional decision to carry me in her womb at the time she did, she was positioning me to be born into a blessed and revolutionary time for Hawaiian people. This timing was a precursor for my current role as a Hawaiian language teacher to Native Hawaiian elders of the English-only generation. This timing was a gift.

I recognize the privileges and gifts I have been afforded each time I walk into my classroom with my class of Hawaiian elders. I have witnessed the tears they shed because of the shame, fear, humiliation, and brutality they have experienced through cultural genocide. Though I did not have to bear that same type of extermination firsthand, I connect so strongly to their feelings because of the experiences in my own household. My grandmother, Kathryne Leilani Labonte, whom I lived with most of my life until she passed in 2013 at the age of 92, shared her similar pain with me. She never developed the ability to speak, read or write in Hawaiian fluently for the same reason as the other elders. I held her hand on many occasions while she cried in both sorrow and anger. Then she would dry her eyes in pride and excitement for me and all that my generation represents in the timeline and revitalization of our culture and people.

Although my grandma did not learn Hawaiian language, she engaged in Hawaiian culture in any way she could. For example, she memorized Hawaiian songs phonetically and sang in a beautiful soprano one voice, accompanied by her 'ukulele[7] strums. Though she did not understand the words, she kept alive that Hawaiian poetry for the next generation who then rediscovered its meanings. She also farmed dozens of acres as did her Hawaiian ancestors. Similarly, my students come with so many wonderful experiences of being Hawaiian and living in a Hawaiian way. They were fortunate to live close to the land and eat her natural foods, stay connected to both immediate and extended family in ways that are difficult to do so today, and live by a code of reciprocity and interdependent relationships that are now often severed by the perceived necessity for speed, independence, and self-preservation.

My students are anything but void of Hawaiian identity and culture. However, an assimilation and erasure process has taken a toll on my elders and often they do not recognize the dazzling Hawaiianness within them. Therefore, I recognize that I am not merely their Hawaiian language teacher. My privilege, as a product of the Hawaiian renaissance – fed by the wisdom of my grandmother, shaped by the brilliance of my mother, and prepared as an academic to deconstruct and dismantle colonization to help heal our people – positions me to bring much more. Therefore, while the class is an introduction to Hawaiian language, we not only learn how to speak Hawaiian, but we also collectively discuss, analyze, and critique areas including but not limited to the education system, politics in Hawai'i and throughout the world, history as we know it and reconstruct it, childhood stories they are now just making sense of, and feelings they have long suppressed and discounted.

In order to do this work together, it is critical that we create a safe, gracious and inviting place for all of us (Hughes, Ruder, & Nienow, 2011). Kindness and empathy are key so that the elders feel comfortable to be open with me, themselves, and each other. In essence, we build aloha. Aloha is defined by Pukui and Elbert (1986) as 'love, affection, compassion, mercy, sympathy, pity, kindness, sentiment, grace, charity' (p. 21). My experience is that aloha is the result of the reciprocal nourishing and caring of one another. Hence, I nourish the group with knowledge of Hawaiian language and care for them with kindness. At the same time, I also invite them to nourish the group with their own knowledge, experiences, and stories and share their values and practices of caring for one another. This caring shows up in ways such as being patient with one other as they try new Hawaiian phrases out loud, celebrating each other's birthdays, gently helping each other through the Hawaiian lessons, and often bringing food to share. These are all ways that the group builds aloha.

For many of them, they will say their first complete sentences in Hawaiian publicly in my class. The idea of doing this in front of their peers is extremely frightening for them. Therefore, I always start the first class of each semester the same way. We sit in a circle and I begin by introducing myself. I tell the story of how I learned Hawaiian and that I recognize how fortunate I am. I follow up by saying, 'But I am still learning like all of you. I don't know everything there is to know about Hawaiian language. I still learn new things everyday like when I am trying to remind my daughter to "flush the toilet" in Hawaiian. So in this class, we are all on a journey of learning together.' They always laugh at the joke about my daughter. At the same time, I also see a hesitant smile of reassurance appear on their faces, calming some of their worries about lack of Hawaiian knowledge and experience. I remind them, we are all recovering from intergenerational trauma (Minton, personal communication, ongoing); that we did not ask for our language and culture to be stripped from us. I remind them that it is not their fault. And then I tell them the story of my grandmother. I end by saying that we are all healing (Minton, personal communication, ongoing) and I invite them to heal with me in our class together.

Then I invite each of them to share their stories. This inevitably takes the entire class period and continues throughout the semester. Many of them cry and tremble in sorrow and frustration regarding their past experiences with or without Hawaiian language in their lives. However, without fail, they each also talk about experiences that teach the rest of us about being Hawaiian and living in a Hawaiian way. When they share those stories, I call it out. I name it (Freire, 1993) as a beautiful contribution to what we know about being Hawaiian. This shift in framework, from deficits to assets, is key for how they view themselves as Hawaiians and how they come to class with more confidence and willingness to reclaim their ancestral connections.

Purposeful storytelling

As academics, parents, and community members, we (Bubba and I) are intentional about each of the stories we tell and how we deliver them (Chi'XapKaid, 2005). In particular, we utilize the stories of our lives to teach, learn, lead, and research through critical self-reflection. Guajardo, Guajardo, and Casaperalta (2008) describe this reflective ethnographic methodology, 'As the observed become part of the observing process, we use a different ontological reality that is congruent with the local ecology and its people yet distant enough where we can be reflective …' (p. 8). We draw from our lives and experiences that are intertwined with those of our communities to teach, learn, lead and research with and for our communities. We recognized that there is great knowledge and power right where we are from and in our daily lives. Hence, we are purposeful about sharing the story of the elders presented above because it illuminates the epistemological, ontological, and pedagogical foundations of our work as it plays out in real life.

We also choose to teach and learn through stories because that is the pedagogical practice passed down to us through our Indigenous ancestral DNA[8] (Kanahele, 2012). Our peoples, for generations, have been teaching, learning, and researching through stories (Kame'eleihiwa, 1996; Lipe, 2013; Wilson, 2008).

For example, in Hawaiian the word for story is moʻolelo, which derives from two Hawaiian words. The first is moʻo, which is translated as 'succession, series, especially a genealogical line, lineage' (p. 253). Moʻo is also described as each vertebra connecting the spine together. The second word, ʻōlelo, translates into English as 'language, speech, word, statement, utterance; to speak, say, converse' (Pukui & Elbert, 1986, p. 284). Therefore, moʻolelo describes the process of connecting life through words.

Noted Hawaiian scholar Mary Kawena Pukui (1983) transcribed a famous Hawaiian proverb, 'I ka ʻōlelo nō ke ola, i ka ʻōlelo nō ka make' (p. 129). Translated literally, this means that 'in speech there is life and in speech there is death' (Pukui, 1983, p. 129). Therefore, not only do Hawaiians place a heavy importance on moʻolelo, but specifically moʻolelo as they are spoken. Because Hawaiian language was a completely oral language until the mid 1800s (Benham & Heck, 1998) it makes sense that ʻōlelo was given so much emphasis and power, as the livelihood of the Hawaiian people – our entire knowledge system – depended on the continuance of moʻolelo.

Moʻolelo Aku, Moʻolelo Mai methodology

Moʻolelo does not exist in isolation, however. The word itself teaches us that it comes to life when spoken and shared. Therefore, moʻolelo aku[9] refers to the sharing of moʻolelo with another. Moʻolelo mai[10] refers to receiving a story. Hence, the methodology of moʻolelo aku moʻolelo mai is the sharing – giving and receiving – of stories (Lipe, 2014). The methodology emphasizes the connections made and preserved through moʻolelo and the power of sharing those moʻolelo with each other by listening and hearing, internalizing, learning, and then re-telling with accuracy.

The significance of interconnectivity and exchange in moʻolelo aku moʻolelo mai is also illuminated in Freire's (1993) dialogical process. According to Freire (Freire & Macedo, 1995):

> In order to understand the meaning of the dialogical practice, we have to put aside the simplistic understanding of dialogue as a mere technique … dialogue characterizes an epistemological relationship … dialogue is a way of knowing and should never be viewed as a mere tactic to involve students in a particular task. We have to make this point very clear. I engage in dialogue not necessarily because I like the person. I engage in dialogue because I recognize the social and not merely the individualistic character of the process of knowing. In this sense, dialogue presents itself as an indispensible component of the process of both learning and knowing. (p. 379)

Therefore, as Freire points out, the interchange of moʻolelo aku moʻolelo mai is key in the interdependent processes of learning and teaching that characterizes our work.

ʻAʻaliʻi Kū Makani framework

We intentionally present the story of elders to provide an example of the work we are committed to. One way to describe the 'work' is to do so through the ʻAʻaliʻi Kū Makani Framework (Lipe, 2014). The ʻAʻaliʻi is a Hawaiian shrub that is often known by the Hawaiian proverb, 'He ʻaʻaliʻi Kū makani mai au, ʻaʻohe makani nāna e kūlaʻi. I am the wind withstanding ʻaʻaliʻi. No gale can push me over' (Pukui, 1983, p. 60). This proverb is further described by Pukui (1983), 'A boast meaning "I can hold my own even in the face of difficulties." The ʻaʻaliʻi bush can stand the worst of gales, twisting and bending but seldom breaking off or falling over' (p. 60). Hence, the ʻAʻaliʻi Kū Makani (Wind-withstanding ʻaʻaliʻi) framework describes a type of leader who personifies the qualities of the ʻaʻaliʻi plant (Figures 1 and 2).

Our work is committed to helping shape those human ʻaʻaliʻi through various forms of educational engagement. First, as the ʻaʻaliʻi is rooted in its island home of Hawaiʻi, we seek to shape leaders who are deeply rooted in the places they call home. We use moʻolelo aku moʻolelo mai (storytelling and conversation) to help folks connect to their home by sharing their own experiences and critically reflecting on those stories. We also make space and create opportunities for folks to engage in the Indigenous values, practices, and knowledge systems of their places. In the example of the class of elders, learning Hawaiian is a way they can become further rooted in who they are by connecting to their ancestral language. At the same time, by sharing stories, they begin to hear their own experiences out loud and those of others and recognize the rootedness they may have previously discounted.

Figure 1. 'A'ali'i cluster.

Figure 2. 'A'ali'i tree blowing in the wind.

Second, as the 'a'ali'i's trunk grows strong yet flexible and is able to withstand high winds and periods of drought (Native Hawaiian Plants, 2009), we help to shape leaders by providing them with experiences to stand firm in their rootedness *and* have expansive minds. Much of our work is providing the space for folks to make connections between their many skills and knowledge systems so that they can use all of that to best serve their environments, families, and communities. In the case of the Hawaiian language class for elders, as we engage in conversation and share stories, they begin to realize how their experiences growing up in their tight-knit communities, learning to sing and play Hawaiian instruments, being punished in the educational system, and fishing with their grandparents are all integral to the resilient Hawaiian people they are today. Then they use all of that positive energy to give them confidence to learn to speak Hawaiian which propels them towards greater pride in being Hawaiian and contributing back to their Hawaiian communities.

Finally, just as the 'a'ali'i has many uses, including how the wood is used for canoes and weapons and tools and posts, the flowers used for lei,[11] the seeds used for dye, and the leaves used for medicine (Native Hawaiian Plants, 2009), we help to celebrate and cultivate the many gifts within each person because of that rootedness and flexibility. Hence, we help folks identify opportunities to use their assets to create and transform the world with their intelligence, strength, and resiliency.

In short, this is our work: to help shape 'a'ali'i kū makani transformative leaders. Many times our work is with young people who are beginning to blossom in so many ways. The story of the elders is an example of our work to make space for more seasoned 'a'ali'i to continue to grow later in their life cycle. Though older, they are always looking for ways to become further rooted in Hawai'i, more expansive in their minds, and sharper with their tools. We see it as an honor to be a part of their continued growth.

A family commitment

Another reason we share the story of the elders is to demonstrate how we have committed to our work as a family. While I (Kaiwipuni) am teaching class on Saturdays, Bubba sets up a picnic in the back of the room for our two children. His main responsibility is to help keep the children quiet yet engaged so the elders can hear and concentrate. Our children listen in on the class, eat snacks, and color in their coloring books or put a puzzle together. They also sometimes play outside, go down to the lo'i,[12] and catch fish in the stream. When they are in the room, they are also included in the class just as children are included in a family living room. I often engage in a Hawaiian conversation with our seven-year old daughter to demonstrate a new sentence pattern. Our son frequently walks between the elders' chairs as they lovingly sneak him treats. He also likes to sit on my lap, nurse, and smile at the class. We believe that these are important experiences for our children in which they learn to be respectful of their elders but also loved by them. At the same time, the elders enjoy the children. If the children do not come because they are sick the elders immediately want to know where they are and why I did not bring them. The children give the elders joy and hope for the future. To be clear, our class has created a family as the result of the aloha we build in the reciprocal nourishing and caring. In this setting, Bubba helps to make this all possible.

On other occasions, Bubba leads initiatives, usually related to Traditional Ecological Knowledge (TEK; Berkes, 1999) and Western science (Lipe, 2013) and I take responsibility of the children. For example, recently Bubba has been building partnerships between Native Hawaiian science and engineering students from the university with Hawaiian community land-based organizations. This work of bringing them together to share in assets, resources, and knowledge systems often happens in the evenings and on weekends. Even though it is Bubba's 'work,' I come along with the children to share in the experience. Our children benefit from having the opportunity to engage with the natural environment and create relationships with their new aunties and uncles: university students and community practitioners. Through this shared family commitment to the work, we are collectively establishing a familial network of mentors for our children.

Whatever the situation may be and whichever parent is leading an activity, we have made the conscious decision to enter into our work as a family. This is our shared commitment as husband and wife and our intention to use all of our experiences as a means for raising and educating our children. Much of their 'schooling' happens in these settings. We also recognize the positive energy that children bring to a setting. Adults become more aware of their actions and are inspired by youth. We cannot imagine doing this work alone or without our children.

A couple's survival

While we engage in the work of shaping 'a'ali'i kū makani, we are constantly reflecting in conversation (Guajardo & Guajardo, 2010; Wheatley, 2009) as a couple. Our time spent sharing is especially important as we meet challenges in our paths, particularly within the contentious confines of the university system (Alfred, 2004). During other moments, we share our excitement or new ideas after meeting with a brilliant student or reading alternative literature. In all these conversations, what we have come to realize is that we are also shaping each other as 'a'ali'i kū makani. We are constantly pushing each other to become further rooted, checking each other on our critical consciousness, and uplifting each other to encourage the work. Hence, we recognize that the guiding values and process that shapes us are the same values and processes we use to shape others. This cyclical process is embedded in the process of recognizing and making sense of our genealogies, realizing our roles based on those genealogies, assuming the responsibilities in those roles, and fulfilling the responsibilities by engaging in the work. In order to best describe this process, we share some stories below.

Shaping genealogies

Dr Pualani Kanaka'ole Kanahele (2012), revered Native Hawaiian hula master and scholar, says that our ancestors live within us. She states that the knowledge and experiences of our ancestors are passed down from generation to generation through our DNA. We build on Dr Kanahele's argument by recognizing that not only do our genealogies of biological family live within us and shape us, but so do other genealogies of knowledge systems, mentorship, and experiences. In our late night conversations, as we make sense of our work and seek paths of strength, we realize we descend from many nourishing genealogies.

Kaiwipuni's story

I am privileged to have been exposed to and engaged in many instances that have awakened ancestral knowledge within me and around me. For example, as a child at bedtime, I would drift off into the world of sleep as my mother recounted the amazing stories of our gods and goddesses. Some of my favorite stories include that of Tutu Pele's[13] hot temper, matched by her fiery lava flow, and of Hi'iakaikapoliopele's[14] gifts as both a warrior and a healer. These stories taught me at least two lessons. First, that my ancestors had incredible power and knowledge. Second, that their strength and ability resided in me as their descendent. These stories were critical to my identity formation as a strong, intelligent, capable Hawaiian woman.

Growing up with my maternal grandmother, she reminded me of both her trials and triumphs. In the face of financial poverty, she kept food on the table, a roof over her children's heads, and even sent my mother to a private school. When all other schools failed my uncle and his struggle with dyslexia, my grandmother organized a new school for children needing special assistance with nearly no money but much determination. Her stories instilled in me a resiliency and a responsibility to care for all, not just our immediate family. I learned from her the true meaning of community and aloha.

I have also been influenced by my parents, two brown scholars and activists[15] who have always stood up for what they believed in despite the overwhelming opposition in their paths. I have been shaped by their commitment on the front lines, their academic scholarship, and their confidence to speak out. Witnessing their brilliance and bravery, their quest for social justice has become my own.

I have not only been shaped by the stories and spirit of both my ancestors as well as my immediate family, but also by many of my early educational settings in which Hawaiian ontologies, pedagogies, and epistemologies were a main focus. In my Hawaiian language immersion school experiences, we learned through songs that honored the land and ocean that surrounded us; we learned all the important aspects of the water cycle through traditional chants; and we spoke the same language that our ancestors did, which further connected us to them with each statement that we made.

When I was not in school, I was with my mother at work at the University of Hawai'i at Mānoa, where she is a professor in Hawaiian Studies.[16] Therefore, my education and identity formation as a young Hawaiian was further influenced by my role models at the University; by educated, outspoken, Hawaiian professors; by budding Hawaiian academics who looked like me and who could speak Hawaiian to me. I also stood side by side with these Hawaiian role models on protest lines, at rallies, and at community events fighting for the survival of Hawaiian language, culture, and education. Therefore, from an early age, I believed I would grow up to be an intelligent and strong Hawaiian woman just like my role models.

In addition to my influences at home and at school, I also grew up in a hālau hula[17] and a hālau wa'a.[18] These hālau provided me a canvas for practical application and further immersion in the Hawaiian values and customs I grew up with at home and in school. These hālau were also opportunities for me to further delve into ancestral knowledge, which was made relevant by my teachers for my life in contemporary Hawai'i.

In addition to the many elements of my world that grounded me in being a Hawaiian woman, I have also been nourished by genealogies within the Western academy. Some of my most influential mentors – professors from the academy – invited my confidence to use my own stories, experiences, and Hawaiian cultural knowledge as foundational material to inform and counter colonizing master narratives in education (Freire, 1993). For example, I recall one occasion in which one of my mentors and dissertation committee members suggested to the rest of my committee that they 'Stay out of her way and let her do her thing.' I recognize that this declaration of confidence in me by my mentor has a genealogy of its own; a line of interconnected mentor/mentee relationships that invites and empowers.

As an adult, I have also been shaped by my time witnessing and engaging in active participation within the academy. In particular I have been involved with faculty who do not take 'no' or 'there is no money' as acceptable answers. Instead they analyze budgets, organize conversations, and engage with both administration and the legislature until their voices and needs are heard and addressed. From this genealogy I have learned the power of pushing beyond what I might believe is possible (Hind, personal communication, April 25, 2013) for the good of the greater group and community.

Bubba's story

I was born and raised in a small town in the Pacific Northwest where my family had moved over 60 years prior. I am a descendant of the Cherokee Nation that comes from the eastern part of the United States. My Cherokee family traces from Oregon to Oklahoma. Before Oklahoma many of my family were and still are found throughout North Carolina, Georgia, and Tennessee. I am registered as a Western Band Cherokee, a term imposed upon my people after the forceful removal of many tribes, including Cherokee, to 'Indian Country,' just west of the Mississippi to Oklahoma in 1838. Hence, those Cherokee who were re-located in the west were given the name 'Western Band Cherokee.' This forceful removal is often known as 'The Trail of Tears' (Pevar, 1992).

My great grandparents on my father's side were both very proud and strong Cherokee who lived most of their lives in Oregon after relocating from Oklahoma during the depression. They lived their lives and raised their family of eight children based on the Indigenous values and beliefs that had been passed down to them. One of these core values was to always have compassion for all things.

In order to earn some extra money my Great Grandmother took a job managing a hotel that mostly served the Indigenous people of the area. There was a reservation nearby, hence the large Indigenous population. Even though she was not from that area and was not part of that Native American tribe, she was known by all the local Indigenous families and soon was considered by most as an extended family member. Through her generosity towards others, Great Grandma created lasting relationships with many of the families. When I was young I remember going to my great grandparents' home to visit and a lot of the time they would have visitors. Many of Great Grandma's visitors became my mentors, teaching and sharing with me Traditional Ecological Knowledge.

Although I was not raised in my ancestral homeland on the eastern side of the United States, my family continued our genealogical practice of actively connecting with the natural environment. For my family, the woods have always been home. My earliest memories are being bundled up in my long johns with two coats and going waterfowl hunting with my family. I was three or four years old at the time. We would rise way before dawn and get all of our clothes on and pile into our old stick-shift Chevy truck, the five of us packed in like sardines, and our black lab named Mike in the back. I was just small enough that Dad would carry me on his shoulders down through the grass and across the creek to our duck blind[19] that sat directly between the Alkalai Lake and a shallow pond surrounded by grain fields. We sat in the dark waiting with anticipation for first light when the sky would awaken with the sounds of waterfowl that would begin their trek from the lake to the pond and grain fields for feeding during the day.

This is where my education began. I remember my dad was very strict about what we shot for food and we were taught from a very young age that we could never shoot anything that we could not first identify by sight, sound, and habit. Simply put it was a matter of respect! Learning how to identify bird species was not the only thing I learned over the years hunting with my family in the duck blind. We learned how the world worked and where we fit into it; how the hawks, eagles, and coyote also hunted the same waters as we did and how the rabbits and neotropical bird species used the same vegetation as our duck blind for homes. We were taught that we were all connected and to see the world through a holistic lens where everything has a purpose and is equally important. We learned that we, as humans, are not more important than any other animal.

Using our senses we could connect with the environments through a much deeper relationship than trying to understand what a marsh is by reading it in a book. The connection was a spiritual one that filled all my senses. I can vividly remember the marsh and those experiences brighter and clearer than any HD video. I can smell the rushes and rabbit brush, I can hear the swans running across the water splashing their wings as they try to get enough thrust and lift to fly. I can see the ducks flying in formation and patterns. I can also see and feel the ducks my mom and dad shot, touching their bills and eyeballs after they fell. I remember the webbing of their feet and how soft the feathers felt. I remember how the water glided off the waterproof feathers and wondering how that is possible. Not only do I hold with me these memories, but these first-hand experiences were also the foundation for all of my later university work in the sciences (Figure 3).

In addition to being shaped by my family and the connections they continue to foster with the natural environment, I am very fortunate to have been nourished by the genealogies of many different Native American and Western educators. One of the most influential people over the years has been Dr. Frank Kanawha Lake. Kanawha is from Karuk, Cherokee, and Chicano heritage, and was working as a fish biologist in Northern California when we met. Kanawha was the first person I ever heard talk about environmental science through an Indigenous lens. He also shared with me how hard it was to be an Indigenous person studying Western science. He said what made it hardest for those of us Indigenous scientists who wanted to utilize both TEK and Western science was that we had to not only know the

Figure 3. Bubba with a steelhead on the Rogue River in Oregon.

ins and outs of both knowledge systems but we also had to know how to transit between and communicate across different worldviews. Listening to his stories and being mentored by him over the years validated who I was and the experiences I had growing up out on those lakes.

Another university genealogy that shaped who I am today resulted from the mentorship and work with Dr Judith Vergun at Oregon State University. Under her leadership, a small group of Indigenous graduate students I was a part of had the opportunity to work on the Warm Springs Sustainability Project, an Indigenous community-based action research project that looked at how to incorporate TEK into Western science. Much of what we learned came from listening and talking with mentors within the communities we were working with such as Kanawha, Robin Kimmerer, Dennis Martinez, Mavis Shaw, Bodie Shaw, Morrie Jimenez, Bob Tom, and Tom Happynook. We also had the opportunity to work with these Indigenous mentors by co-teaching a course with Dr Vergun that looked at natural resource science and education through an Indigenous lens. It was this course that changed my life and my thinking about science and how it is taught or not taught in the classrooms. When our group was not teaching we were researching, reading, and discussing issues and ideas about how to build bridges between what we were learning in our Western science courses with the teachings of Indigenous communities. We then took those connections and developed courses, curricula, and presentations that incorporated both Indigenous and Western perspectives in science education. We used this work to engage with K-12 schools, university students and faculty, and also community organizations and Native American tribes.

Many of those Indigenous mentors were telling us to look closer at what was being taught, or more importantly not being taught, in the sciences within the academy. This is when I first started to define who I was as a Cherokee man within the university. I was also learning where my childhood experiences and relationships to the outdoors I had gained over the years fit into Western science.

Reflecting on our genealogies

We both can and have been labeled by others, including academic researchers, as disadvantaged because of our socioeconomic status and because we both come from ethnic backgrounds that are underrepresented in higher education and other areas of economic opportunity. However, as we critically reflect on our genealogical stories in conversation as a couple and with others, we do not define ourselves as disadvantaged. We reject that label. This is the power of the ethnographic methodology defined by Guajardo et al. (2008) as described above. Through research on ourselves, our families, our communities, and our environments, we define ourselves as strong, resilient, and connected. We recognize those assets within us because we acknowledge, reflect, and make sense of the many genealogies that shape us.

The power of place

As is evident within our many genealogical stories, we both have been and continue to be shaped in very unique ways. On a geographical level, I (Kaiwipuni) was raised in my homeland. This reality has privileged me to be actively involved in my Indigenous language and culture. Bubba, on the other hand, was not raised on his ancestral lands because of forced removal (Pevar, 1992). Instead his resilient family brought values and practices embedded in their ancestral DNA (Kanahele, 2012) to their new home. I also spent much of my time in traditional academic institutions, either at my school or at the university with my mother. Bubba spent much of his time in the outdoor academic institution better known as the natural environment. In both our cases, the places where we grew up shaped us in different yet serious ways.

In our work we are careful to engage with others in spaces and places with intention. We recognize the power of the landscapes and ecologies of a place as critical shaping genealogies. For example, we hold our Hawaiian language and culture classes for elders at the university. However, those classes are in no way connected to university coursework and counted within the university system. Our classes are completely independent of the university; we are a community-based non-profit organization who utilizes a university classroom at Kamakakūokalani Center for Hawaiian Studies at the University of Hawai'i at Mānoa.[20] When the elders come each Saturday, they feel a part of the larger Hawaiian education movement because of the location of their classes. In addition, in order to utilize the space, our group is responsible for doing simple cleaning like weeding and plant pruning on site several times a year. In this way, we engage with the natural environment of the place, which allows us to further connect to the space that nourishes us.

Intentional mentorship

Each of us also has mentors from different parts of the world with unique specializations. At the same time, we both connect to genealogies of Indigenous mentorship within the academy and also in the community. It is especially important how different mentors along the way invited and included us in the teaching, learning, leading, and research processes.

We are deliberate about inviting and including our own students and mentees into the learning process with us. Something as simple as 'What graduate programs are you applying for?' invites and expands the imagination of what a student previously thought she was capable of. An inquiry such as 'Tell me the story of how your family hunts deer' recognizes a student's knowledge system that may have never before been of interest from an academic mentor. It is amazing how these simple yet intentional invitations build relationships and opportunities.

Realizing our roles

Our shaping genealogies have prepared us in very significant ways to assume particular roles in our homes, in our communities, and also in the academy. Our personal interests and skill sets also intersect with those genealogies to shape us. One way to describe these emerging roles is to look to the Hawaiian example. Specifically, in the Hawaiian worldview, when we know our genealogies – how we are connected through bloodlines, experiences, knowledge systems, and relationships – the familial order of kaikua'ana and kaikaina is established.

Kaikua'ana refers to the elder sibling or senior genealogical line while kaikaina refers to the younger sibling or junior genealogical line (Pukui & Elbert, 1986). Defining the relationship between the kaikua'ana and kaikaina is kuleana. Some of the English words for kuleana include responsibility, right, privilege, concern, and authority (Pukui & Elbert, 1986). Generations of Hawaiian ancestral knowledge teach us about the interdependent and reciprocal nature of this relationship (Kamakau, 1991; Kame'eleihiwa, 1992).

Specifically, the kuleana of the kaikua'ana is to nourish and protect (Kame'eleihiwa, 1992). For example, in Hawaiian tradition, the land and plants are born before humans (Lili'uokalani, 1897). Those plants feed the people and provide the tools necessary for protection and shelter. In our households we similarly see this responsibility carried out when the elder of the house nourishes the younger members with both food and knowledge and also protects them by providing them with a home.

Interdependently, the kuleana of the kaikaina is to mālama. English terms for mālama include to care for and tend to (Pukui & Elbert, 1986). Returning to the Hawaiian genealogy of the land, plants, and humans, humans are born last and are thus kaikaina to the land and plants. Hence, the kuleana of humans is to care and tend to the land and plants so those natural elements can continue to produce nourishment and protection. In a Hawaiian household, we can recognize this responsibility the way the young ones make sure the elders are well tended to, cared for, and kept comfortable.

With this said, as I (Kaiwipuni) reflect on my many genealogies, the kaikua'ana/kaikaina relationship is especially useful for me as I think about how to engage in the world through a Hawaiian worldview. At the same time, although Bubba did not grow up with these particular Hawaiian concepts, he was raised with very similar roles and responsibilities. He recognizes that he has been nourished and now assumes the role to nourish others. In particular, two contexts in which we now recognize our role as kaikua'ana include the context of parenthood and the context of educator.

Becoming parents

The most relevant context in which we have arrived as the kaikua'ana or the one responsible for nourishing is within the context of becoming parents. This is a journey we have indeed been on together, constantly learning, reflecting, and engaging in conversation with each other, our parents, and other mentors. As parents of two children, our seven-year-old daughter Hā'ena and our four year-old son Lamakū, the conversion of all our genealogies could not be more clear and yet complex. As all parents do, we want everything for our children. Our 'everything' includes all that we have been nourished within our genealogies, including but not limited to Hawaiian language, hula, a critical consciousness, hunting, fishing, and a spiritual connection to mother earth (Figure 4).

In addition, as we get to know their unique personalities, we recognize Hā'ena's love for art, story, and theater and Lamakū's physical strength and agility. We know that their skills and interests will continue to grow and develop. Therefore, we look to our genealogical stories to inform us on how to shape them and recognize that we have to connect with other genealogies when we need help.[21] Undoubtedly, we strive to utilize all that has nourished us – both in the academy and also from our Indigenous knowledge systems – to nourish our own children.

Education beyond our family

As we reflect on our genealogical stories, one of the things that has become evident is that we would not be who we are today if we were only fed by our biological genealogies. Many of our mentors come from outside our families, outside our own cultures, and from across oceans and continents. Therefore, we recognize that part of our responsibility in having been nourished by those different genealogies is continuing the life of that genealogy; we must continue to teach and share beyond our own children.[22] Interdependently, we know that when we nourish our students, we are building a healthier community for our children.

The weight of the responsibility

While our role and responsibility as educators with students and colleagues is both exciting and invigorating, we admit that sometimes it feels overwhelming. Searching for paid work in an academy that does not value our work can be exhausting. Juggling an internal consciousness towards moral courage

Figure 4. Kaiwipuni and daughter Hā'ena performing a hula together.

and the reality of paying rent in Hawai'i can be draining. Sometimes all we want to do is run away to the forests of Oregon or to the beaches on Moloka'i.[23] On occasion, we do sneak out for a few days. Using that time away to rejuvenate, we return to our responsibility to continue our work in the place we have been mentored to occupy: the space in and between the academy and our communities. We recognize the privilege of being a part of genealogies situated within the university setting and also stemming from Indigenous cultural practice. Hence part of our responsibility in our role as educators is to be border crossers, translators, and transitors; to help create the space for more diverse connections and conversations to occur across multiple borders.

Caretaking and stewardship

In addition to coming into our roles as kaikua'ana as parents and mentors, we also recognize that there are some relationships in which we will always be the kaikaina as a student, mentee, and steward. For example, we will always be our parents' children. We are also children of the land and recognize that no matter where we live, mother earth sustains us with each breath we take, each step we tread on her bosom, and each drink of water we consume. As kaikaina, we recognize our role to tend to our elders and senior genealogies by utilizing our Indigenous knowledge as well as our academic skills. With our parents our responsibility can be as simple as ensuring their health, both physical and spiritual, amidst all the distractions and busyness of the world. Within this responsibility we also teach our children how to tend to their grandparents such as by sending them to check that their grandma and grandpa have eaten dinner and making sure to kiss them goodnight.

Our relationship with the land is also critical and sometimes made complicated by our limited access on a daily basis.[24] However, how can we teach about cultural practice and environmental stewardship if we do not live it ourselves? Therefore, through our late night conversations and also partnering with our neighbors and nearby community groups, we find ways to practice our role as stewards of the environment and to teach that value and practice to our children (Figure 5).

On other occasions, we rally with others from the university, our families, and also our communities to protect our land. This sometimes includes sit-ins, protesting, and testifying on behalf of our mother earth.[25] Our recognition of this important role as caretaker is tricky in the world of academia, which often does not value that kind of constant tending and caring required. Also, universities are often

Figure 5. The taro plant (staple food of the Hawaiian people) and our son, Lamakū, learning about how to care for it at Ka Papa Lo'i 'o Kānewai taro garden at the University of Hawai'i at Mānoa.

involved in the desecration of mother earth and our Indigenous sacred places in the name of science and knowledge creation.[26] Hence, we recognize our responsibility as heightened in this role to use multiple pedagogical approaches to help inform and invite academia into our world and value systems to create a shift in consciousness and praxis within the academy for our environments and communities. We have learned and continue to be mentored by elders in our community as we emerge as 'a'ali'i kū makani in this critical area and also begin to shape future 'a'ali'i, including our children and students, who will sustain this work.

Scholarship for our children

We see our role as parents as defining the work we do because ultimately, we are trying to shape the ecology by preparing transformational leaders who will positively impact our children and the many generations yet to come. We look to our students – future educators, scientists, and policy-makers – to be 'a'ali'i kū makani so that they make decisions and engage in praxis (Freire, 1993) that cultivates our children's joys and gifts and sustains the natural environments for future generations. We acknowledge that the academy is a great place to engage in this work because it provides so many opportunities for both mentors and mentees to engage in the teaching and learning process. We also know that higher education benefits our students in multiple ways that afford them promising futures.

Often, however, the academy is slow in its response to knowledge systems, values, methodologies, and genealogies such as our own. Although all universities in Hawai'i and across the United States of America are situated upon Indigenous land (Justice, 2004), the institutions do not descend from genealogies whose values align with those of Indigenous peoples; that are responsive and reciprocal in their aloha to communities and environments. We also recognize that institutions are comprised of people. We believe, because we have witnessed it, that people can change. The example of the elders reminds us that even late in a life cycle people can grow and transform. Hence, we have hope for our university and others like it that they can become populated with more 'a'ali'i kū makani who can transform the campus culture (Jayakumar & Museus, 2012) to reflect Indigenous values and ways of knowing and being.

We recognize that our genealogies put us in a position to help shift the consciousness of the academy. We believe that the principles and values that have guided our own journeys and arrival – the critical reflection through auto-ethnographic research including the connecting and sense making of our genealogies and the recognizing of our resulting roles and responsibilities – can also shape and transform those who comprise the university. While we want to become professors at our university so that we can work with students, other faculty, and engage in the process of research and knowledge creation with community, that is not our current reality. I (Kaiwipuni) am in a temporary one-year non-teaching faculty position and Bubba's position at the university is terminating with the end of a grant cycle. However, that does not mean that the work stops. When we look at our children, we are reminded that we must be more creative. There is not a minute to lose. We also know from our own experiences that the academy is not the only place where 'a'ali'i kū makani can be nourished and cultivated. The community is fertile ground. Therefore we engage in this work where and with the people we have access to: our children, families, and communities. As we do so, we invite the academy into this work through various partnerships so that they can witness and be transformed by our engaged scholarship for our children and communities.

Notes

1. The authors of this piece are husband and wife and together have two children.
2. Likelike is a Hawaiian word (pronounced Lee-kay lee-kay).
3. In 1893 a small group of white businessmen performed a coup d'état and overthrew Queen Lili'uokalani, the reigning Hawaiian monarch (Lili'uokalani, 1897).

4. In 1983 less than 1% of all Hawaiians could speak Hawaiian and there were approximately 500 native speakers left. Today, 3–5% of Hawaiians can now speak Hawaiian. Therefore, there has been a increase in the last 30 years and yet there is still much work to do.
5. Hula: Hawaiian dance.
6. Her dissertation was later published as the book Kame'eleihiwa (1992).
7. An 'ukulele is a Hawaiian musical instrument resembling a small guitar.
8. Kaiwipuni is Native Hawaiian and Bubba is Western-Band Cherokee. We will describe this in more detail later in the piece.
9. Aku: 'Expressing direction away from the speaker' (Pukui & Elbert, 1986, p. 15).
10. Mai: 'Towards the speaker, this way' (Pukui & Elbert, 1986, p. 220).
11. Lei: Garland, wreath; necklace of flowers, leaves, shells, ivory, feathers, or paper, given as a symbol of affection (Pukui & Elbert, 1986).
12. A lo'i is a Hawaiian taro garden that is fed by streams. There is a lo'i adjacent to the building where our class is held.
13. Tutu Pele is the affectionate name my family (and many others) gives to Pele, the Hawaiian goddess responsible for volcanoes, lava, and new land (Handy & Pukui, 1998; Kame'eleihiwa, 1999).
14. Hi'iakaikapoliopele is a Hawaiian goddess who is famed for her ability to battle large dragons and also bring someone back to life (Ho'oulumāhiehie, 1905–1906).
15. My father, Dr James Anthony, is a Fiji born East Indian. He earned his PhD in History from Australia National University. My mother, Dr Lilikalā Kame'eleihiwa, is a Hawaiian academic. She earned her PhD in History from the University of Hawai'i at Mānoa.
16. My parents divorced when I was six years old and I grew up primarily with my mom.
17. Hālau hula: A hula school.
18. Hālau wa'a: Canoe paddling school.
19. A duck blind is a place where we hide from the ducks while we hunt them.
20. For more information and photographs of this building, visit http://manoa.hawaii.edu/hshk/kamakakuokalani/
21. Examples include early childhood education and development and social entrepreneurialship. These are not our areas of expertise yet we see the value and importance of them so we partner with others who are experts to stregthen the work we do.
22. We recognize that there is knowledge that should be kept within the family and knowledge that can be shared out. We also recognize that our mentors who are not from our own families teach and share certain things only with their own families and other things with mentees such as ourselves. Therefore, when we suggest cotinuing the genealogy of mentorship and knowlege from our mentors, we mean it in the sense that is appropriate and does not defy any type of familial privacy.
23. Moloka'i is a small island within the Hawaiian archipelago. It is still very rural and has beautiful places to return to a more traditional way of living close to the land.
24. We live in a town house with a front-yard that is 4 feet by 8 feet and a small backyard on a steep slope. Hence, there is not much space to interact with the natural environment within the vicinity of our house.
25. In Hawai'i, especially, there is constant overdevelopment and devastation to our natural environments and resources in the name of tourism and Western science. There are many land struggles to cite. A current issue right now is the desecration of the Hawaiian sacred mountain Mauna Kea to build a 30-meter telescope.
26. The academy uses science and knowledge creation as the reason for desecration of sacred sites is necessary though we know from both experience and research that Indigenous science and knowledge creation has occurred for generations in harmony with the environment rather than by destroying it.

Disclosure statement

No potential conflict of interest was reported by the authors.

References

'Aha Pūnana Leo. (2015). *A timeline of revitalization*. Retrieved from http://www.ahapunanaleo.org/index.php?/about/a_timeline_of_revitalization/

Alfred, T. (2004). Warrior scholarship: Seeing the university as a ground of contention. In D. A. Mihesuah & A. C. Wilson (Eds.), *Indigenizing the academy: Transforming scholarship and empowering communities* (pp. 88–99). Lincoln: University of Nebraska Press.

Benham, M. K. P., & Heck, R. H. (1998). *Culture and educational policy in Hawai'i: The silencing of native voices*. Mahwah, NJ: Lawrence Erlbaum.

Berkes, F. (1999). *Sacred ecology: Traditional ecological knowledge and resource management*. Philadelphia, PA: Taylor & Francis.

Chi'XapKaid. (2005). Decolonizing through storytelling. In W. A. Wilson & M. Yellow (Eds.), *For indigenous eyes only: A decolonization handbook* (pp. 127–138). Santa Fe, New Mexico: School of American Research Press.

Freire, P. (1993). *Pedagogy of the oppressed*. New York, NY: Continuum International.

Freire, P., & Macedo, D. (1995). A dialogue: Culture, language, and race. *Harvard Educational Review, 65*, 377–403.

Guajardo, F., & Guajardo, M. (2010). Cultivating stories of change. In K. Ruder (Ed.), *The collective leadership storybook: Weaving strong communities* (pp. 85–104). Seattle, WA: The Center for Ethical Leadership.

Guajardo, M., Guajardo, F., & Casaperalta, E. (2008). Transformative education: Chronicling a pedagogy for social change. *Anthropology & Education Quarterly, 39*, 3–22. doi:10.1111/j.1548-1492.2008.00002.x

Handy, E. S. C., & Pukui, M. K. (1998). *The Polynesian family system in Ka'ū, Hawai'i*. Honolulu, HI: Mutual Publishing.

Ho'oulumāhiehie. (1905–1906). Ka mo'olelo o Hi'iakaikapoliopele. *Ka Na'i Aupuni*.

Hughes, P. M., Ruder, K., & Nienow, D. (2011). *Courageous collaboration with gracious space: From small openings to profound transformation*. Seattle, WA: Center for Ethical Leadership.

Jayakumar, U. M., & Museus, S. (2012). Mapping the intersection of campus cultures and equitable outcomes among racially diverse student populations. In S. Museus & U. M. Jayakumar (Eds.), *Creating campus cultures: Fostering success among racially diverse student populations* (pp. 1–27). New York, NY: Routledge.

Justice, D. H. (2004). Seeing (and reading) red: Indian outlaws in the ivory tower. In D. A. Mihesuah & A. C. Wilson (Eds.), *Indigenizing the academy: Transforming scholarship and empowering communities* (pp. 100–123). Lincoln: University of Nebraska Press.

Kanahele, P. K. (2012, February 4). *Ho'omālamalama o nā wahine kapu*. Presentation at 'Aha Wahine, Windward Community College, Kāne'ohe.

Kamakau, S. M. (1991). *Ruling chiefs of Hawaii*. Honolulu: Kamehameha Schools Press.

Kame'eleihiwa, L. (1992). *Native land and foreign desires*. Honolulu, HI: Bishop Museum Press.

Kame'eleihiwa, L. (1996). *A legendary tradition of Kamapua'a – The Hawaiian pig-god*. Honolulu, HI: Bishop Museum Press.

Kame'eleihiwa, L. (1999). *Nā wahine kapu: Divine Hawaiian women*. Honolulu, HI: 'Ai Pōhaku Press.

Kamins, R. M. (1998). Origins and early years: 1907–1946. In R. M. Kamins & R. E. Potter (Eds.), *Mālamalama – A history of the University of Hawai'i* (pp. 3–51). Honolulu, HI: University of Hawai'i Press.

Lili'uokalani. (1897). *An account of the creation of the world according to Hawaiian tradition*. Boston, MA: Lee and Shepard.

Lipe, D. (2013). *Diversifying science: Recognizing indigenous knowledge systems as scientific worldviews* (Doctoral dissertation). University of Hawai'i at Mānoa, Honolulu, HI.

Lipe, K. (2014). *Aloha as fearlessness: Lessons from the mo'olelo of eight Native Hawaiian female educational leaders on transforming the University of Hawai'i at Mānoa into a Hawaiian place of learning* (Doctoral dissertation). University of Hawai'i at Mānoa, Honolulu, HI.

Pevar, S. L. (1992). *The rights of Indians and tribes: The basic ACLU guide to Indian and tribal rights*. Carbondale: Southern Illinois University Press.

Pukui, M. K. (1983). *'Olelo no'eau*. Honolulu, HI: Bishop Museum Press.

Pukui, M. K., & Elbert, S. H. (1986). *Hawaiian dictionary*. Honolulu, HI: University of Hawai'i Press.

Trask, H. K. (1992). *Welcoming address for the Hawaiian Studies building groundbreaking – October 27, 1992*. Honolulu, HI: Center for Hawaiian Studies, University of Hawai'i at Mānoa. Unpublished manuscript.

Wheatley, M. J. (2009). *Turning to one another: Simple conversations to restore hope to the future*. San Francisco, CA: Berrett-Koehler.

Wilson, S. (2008). *Research is ceremony: Indigenous research methods*. Black Point: Fernwood.

We help each other up: Indigenous scholarship, survivance, tribalography, and sovereign activism

Lee Francis IV, Michael M. Munson and their Communities

ABSTRACT

In an academic system that perpetuates the control and limitation of Indigenous narrative in order to reinforce the Western settler-colonial framework, Francis and Munson aim to create a more appropriate space for Indigenous scholarship. Through conversation, the authors discuss the exploration of sovereign scholar activism through an Indigenous autoethnographic approach. Tribalography, Survivance, and creation and experiential stories of home serve as fuel for the examination of identity, community, and authenticity in the formation of a framework built upon the scholarship of Indigenous researchers, conversations, and experiences since time immemorial. Questions are posed to continue and broaden the conversation toward actualizing a state of sovereign scholarship and the entrenchment of Tribalography and Survivance as means of establishing an Indigenous scholarship free from the confines of settler-colonialism.

Invocation

Da-aah Mehyuu-nah Nuudeh-guyah Sru'tsa

Steh-gaadzeh yukeh kaatyah-stih nuwaakameh-eh sru'tsah.

Nieukah-chana sru'tsah, guwaa unah-kaatya srahanu tyiemeeshi dzeh-ehmishee,

guwaa dzieu-kai-ih-tishii, guwaa sramee-dzeh-ehmeeshi

Duweh waitsih hanu stutah-ah-tehsi, emeh eh nyieu-kai-ih sru-tsah.

Eehmih eh heyah sramee eh dawaa eh niwautra-skuwaadrumah.

Keemuu ehmih eh yuuni ganaatah'si

Dawaah eh aneh eh, dawaah eh aneh eh dzah.

Tuu dyuutrusrah dawaah eh aneh eh, nu daa guh.

This Is The Way Still We Shall Go On

It is necessary to look back to the past.

Gazing we will see how our peoples in the past lived,

how they were guided, how they lived well.

We who are living today, that is what we are to be guided by.

That is the way of living that will be correct and good for us.

As you know, that is what the song says:

Good and beautiful, good and beautiful it is.

Always it will be good and beautiful, it will be. (Ortiz, 2002, p. 92)

Introduction

Our work together began in Philadelphia in 2013. We met through a colleague at the big educational conference. As Indigenous[1] PhD students, we found ourselves in conversation with some of our academic 'heroes' during a large academic conference. Over the course of several days, we began to realize we faced similar challenges as emerging Indigenous scholars searching for our identities within the academy. We shared numerous stories about the obstacles and barriers that existed in a system that was not designed to accommodate Indigenous ways of knowing and being. We discussed the incongruous nature of our scholarship that was offered limited space when that scholarship contained the authenticity and integrity of an Indigenous framework. We felt constrained in developing innovative qualitative research that remained true to our home communities as we felt the standard academic approaches continued to serve as a means of controlling the Indigenous narrative and reinforcing the Western settler-colonial framework.

And so, we began a conversation that stretched throughout the next year (and continues on to this day). What emerged was the foundation for this document. It was the exploration of sovereign scholar activism through an Indigenous autoethnographic approach. It was the examination of identity, community, and authenticity. It was the formation of a framework built upon the scholarship of Indigenous researchers since time immemorial. Our conversations were informal and built upon the stories of our experiences. These stories featured similar themes and understandings that were present in the Indigenous communities we called home: Lee from the Pueblo of Laguna and Michael from Salish-Pend d'Orielle territory in Western Montana.

From our stories emerged two concepts that served as a guide for this work: Tribalography and Survivance. Tribalography is the reorientation of narratives and conceptual approaches that place Indigenous knowledge and perspectives at the center (Howe, 1999). Survivance is the combination of survival and resistance that moves Indigenous people from colonial victims to agents of power and intention (Vizenor, 1994). The synthesis of these concepts highlights our experiences as emerging scholars and our journey in the development of our scholar activism. As the purpose of scholarship is to engage, articulate, and propel ideas, knowledge, and theories, we must assert 'the inseparable relationship between story and knowing, and the interrelationship between narrative and research within Indigenous frameworks. In considering story as both method and meaning, it is presented as a culturally nuanced way of knowing' (Kovach, 2005, p. 94). We have come to realize our scholarship is different and as such is presented differently. As Pueblo writer Leslie Marmon Silko explains,

> For those of you accustomed to being taken from point A to point B to point C, this presentation may be somewhat difficult to follow. Pueblo expression resembles something like a spider's web – with many little threads radiating from the center, crisscrossing each other. As with the web, the structure emerges as it is made and you must simply listen and trust … that meaning will be made. (Silko, 1981, p. 1)

This document then is a weaving, as web, a way of synthesizing and presenting our scholarship as to align with the Indigenous philosophical frameworks we both bring to our work. It is a weaving of stories, conversations, reflections, and memories. It is echoes of past, present, and future; told sometimes as story, sometimes as conversation, sometimes as a blending of the words of our ancestors, elders, and mentors. We do not do this alone but seek to present our understandings as derived from our relationships will all that has come before us and all that will come after us (Cajete, 1994; Francis, 2001; Smith, 2011). What we demonstrate, in this work, is the conversation of two storytellers,[2] who are looking to the past to guide our actions in the future; to show how we can be good and beautiful, authentic and intentional, and ultimately how we can give back the blessings we have received, which we view as part of our responsibility as sovereign scholars. As a Pueblo elder and colleague states:

> The phrase 'hon e:beya tsu:ma, e:yakna tho'o" means to hold strongly to each other so we may grow in our relations and collective strength now and for the future. This hope and instruction is depicted on the walls of the Grand Canyon. As the A:shiwi emerged from the fourth world there is a depiction of two human (A:shiwi) figures. One is on the surface with hand extended grasping the hand of another and pulling him/her to the surface and into the present world. As A:shiwi people, we must learn to practice this in all areas of life and relations. (Lewis, 2012, personal correspondence)

Indigenous sovereign activism

As Brayboy (2006) notes in his work on Tribal Critical Theory, 'colonization is endemic to society' (p. 439) and therefore exists in all spaces of Indigenous practice. This is certainly true within higher education institutions, where research and scholarship are prized above all else; a privileged Western research that values and validates itself to the exclusion of other frameworks of understanding. This is evident in the number of dissertations, articles, and conversations by Indigenous scholars who find they are forced to outline the Indigenous framework, in the same way, or else face questions regarding validity and merit during the review process. It seems absurd that Indigenous scholars have been writing strong academic work that outlines the tenants of Indigenous philosophy for more than 50 years, yet Indigenous scholars are still required to defend the methodology as if it is some sort of abnormal approach. Therefore, the need to continue to pursue the idea of sovereignty within the academy is critical to the development of the Indigenous scholar, as 'the mind cannot function effectively if it is imprisoned. An intelligentsia cannot exist if the minds of the people are programmed to accept whatever colonialism decrees' (Forbes, 1980, p. 84).

The idea of sovereignty is complex and wrought with colonial ideology (Russell, 2010), though the concept has also been subverted by Indigenous people to hold deeper meaning that reflects survival, perseverance, ceremony, tradition, and celebration (Armstrong, 2000; Vizenor, 1994). For the purpose of this article, we hold to the notion of sovereignty and the sovereign intellect that has been outlined by the Lenape scholar, Forbes (1998), who stated that sovereignty should be a 'a state we achieve through a steady struggle for self-determination, a result of many cumulative decisions that we make for ourselves as we move toward self-governance and intellectual self-direction' (p. 15). Enacting this type of sovereign scholarship, then, requires a different way of thinking about this work and its approaches. Instead of a linear narrative that moves from A to B, we see this as a weaving, a web that speaks to the multiplicity of Indigenous, Native American, Aboriginal and First Nations communities and experiences. It encompasses an array of shared understandings among Indigenous peoples with the full awareness that the scholarship should continue to evolve especially as globalization has afforded a dialogic interchange among Indigenous peoples throughout the world.

And so, we begin our conversation:

Lee: What is your definition of sovereign activism?

Michael: Well, I think, we're activists for our own community, right? So we have sovereignty to do what's needed for and with our people and for all of our generations to come. In my mind, it's all about building the skills of our students and the opportunities for our students to do whatever is needed – to become more, and more, and more sovereign. Even though sovereignty is totally a dominant term right …

Lee: Right.

Michael: But within the confines of that word, I think serving absolutely as an activist – as a tool or a bridge between the government system, the federal government system and our own communities in order for our communities to find sovereignty. That's probably my most concise definition. If you wanna just capture that one right there, that's probably the best one.

Lee: No, I think that's … I think that's, that lines right up … I'm looking at the idea of sovereign activism and I think it's also about reminding our own people and demonstrating to the outsider, whoever that may be, demonstrating to them the ways in which we did and continue to do things, the being and knowing, is just as important. So this idea, that we can demonstrate by our actions a different way of approaching, say research or scholarship or stories, or, you know, community development in a way that's appropriate and authentic? It reminds me of a story out of Zuni, their origin story, their creation story in the petroglyphs was about that they were helping each other out from the underground place, where they emerged from. So they were pulling and the idea was that they would pull each other out to become, to come to this place of the light, this place of being. So that is a Core value of an Indigenous process, that idea of … it becomes sovereign activism, right? Moving towards an authenticity as a confluence of all the knowledge supports and all the things throughout time immemorial. And I know that others have talked about the centering around values as a key to a sovereign activism, at least for me.

Michael: Absolutely, and I think those values are common threads: humility, honesty, courage, truth, love, honor, and respect. I don't know what your guys' are, but I bet you they're really similar. I bet you we have those common values, those common threads.

Lee: Yeah, ours are similar. So in some ways it's an alternative to the mainstream, right? So from that perspective, I am curious as to what that kind of scholarship may have looked like? How would that have been 'in the field' three hundred years ago? What was the concept of scholarship at that point? In other words, what is our scholarship tradition or our historical continuum of scholarship for Indigenous people?

Michael: Right. Well, from what I've been taught, dreams are very … dreams and knowledge that *comes* to you is very legitimate. There's a connection to the spiritual world in that way. And I know it seems fancy or mystified but I definitely think it's important. And as a result of that observation, learning to work with, to work with our ecological surroundings is important, also. So observation, and you can even say that people, people would say that the way that they interacted with the environment – the flora, the fauna, or whatever was surrounding them, and the other people that were with them. So, the process of observation, of learning to identify different things, like, ant hills … the science of ant hills determine how strong the winter would be. Those are all sources of knowledge.

Lee: Yeah. I think also the ways in which meaning was made was approached differently, more communally. The research would have been for the community and by the community, not for the individual. It would have been in a council type meeting or it would have been in a clan meeting or it would have been in a particular setting where these modes would have been all brought together. There would have been one conduit point where everything would have been made, where everything, where the individual would bring their own meanings so then the community could then construct meaning out of that. Which I think is one of the things that is so critical in terms of the work that Indigenous scholars do is that it has to be bound in community and with community, right? So it has to be both. It's the opposite of Western academics, which is about the individual. The individual researcher makes meaning on behalf of the researched.

Michael: Absolutely! We have Salish and Pend d'Oreille Culture and Committee meetings where we have an Elder Advisory Council. So there's one, two, three, four, five, six, seven, eight, nine, ten, eleven, about twelve elders who are Salish and Pend d'Oreille. Both men and women who represent various families with knowledge and who have language, which is something that we don't have very many people who have those things anymore. So the way the meeting is run, is various people form the community come to the elders and they seek advice. They seek guidance. They seek answers to problems that they're dealing with, either in the health care system, tribal historic preservation, in education, whatever the case may be. So people are coming to present on the work they are doing within the tribe for our people or with our people, depending on the situation. And they are seeking guidance for that. So, they're in community and they're trying to find solutions with the elders, from the elders, with the elders in a community-based setting where all of the public is invited to attend. And to provide guidance, as well, right? With the elders being the primary knowledge keepers. So, seeing those processes continue over and over and over, every month, where there's a space for dialogue, there's a space for working with community. There's a space for bringing knowledge through story. Usually, many of the elders use stories from their past. From their yayá?s and síle?s and qéne?s and t̓úpye?s, right? From their ancestors … that are brought forth to the issues that we're dealing with within our community and within our environment right now.

Lee: Right.

Michael: And so that constant process of dialogue, of give and take, of reciprocation between each of the elders, but also within the community members and how that interaction plays out, is really interesting. Rather than with me being in the central role. And that's our contribution as Indigenous scholars, as Indigenous activist scholars: to continue that process with the constant understanding about what is right for our communities from … not from us, but from our communities.

Lee: Exactly! I think the approach or strategy of reorienting our knowledge to the center of our scholarship is critical in demonstrating sovereign activism. It moves the narrative away from the individual Western constructs to a more collectivist and authentic representation of knowledge, research, and scholarship in which Indigenous stories and voices are given the authority to represent themselves rather than having to be positioned beside Western scholars or scholarship in order to be validated. I think that is what Howe was ultimately trying to accomplish when she articulated the notion of tribalography: a repositioning of story in order to generate a new discourse with the mainstream intelligencia.

Tribalography

As we began to tell more stories relating to the churches and missionaries, the non-Indians became defensive. One woman in the audience asked if we couldn't think of at least one good thing the Catholic church had done for Indians. Others began to tell their stories: the Jewish Holocaust, of the horrors of slavery and what was done to African Americans, the hardships that the Italians and the Irish had faced at Ellis Island. What I believe was happening to the non-Indians was that they were threading their lives and experiences into ours. A shift in paradigm, it's generally believed to be the other way around: Indians assimilating into the mainstream … we kept on talking through dinner, until I thought my head was unraveling … in my story, all this interaction, and yes resolution to change our perspectives, to change ourselves. (Howe, 1999, p. 124)

The centering of Indigenous knowledge and stories is a process and concept developed by Choctaw playwright and scholar, LeAnne Howe. Termed Tribalography, it is a way of positioning and validating Indigenous story by situating Indigenous stories as central components in a way that disrupts colonial binaries and allows for authentic dialogue and engagement. Tribalography draws the focus on the story of the Indigenous experience as a central starting point rather than as an addition to the mainstream narrative. As Howe noted previously, when Indigenous people reclaim and promote their perspectives and stories, it has the tendency to make non-Natives uncomfortable, as it does not adhere to the strict settler-colonial narrative. Yet, Tribalography doesn't simply flip the dynamic as some type of counter-narrative, rather it deconstructs the binary by focusing on the story and the totality of the experience of Indigenous people – past, present, and future. This shift in positioning has an unsettling effect on those who have chosen or been forced to take up the role of the colonizer. The space is disrupted because the focus is on the story; the story is allowed to expand. At the core are Indigenous experiences but now they are woven with others in a way that highlights the fluidity and power of stories made manifest. The concept of diplomacy and invitation then form and develop, 'In stark contrast to the binary between the colonizer and the colonized, Howe's retellings of Choctaw history emphasize flexibility and diplomacy as modes of intertribal interaction' (Horan & Kim, 2013, p. 31). Rather than a conflictual approach, Tribalography shifts the paradigm in a way that allows for equity and dignity, all the while subverting the conceived notions of history, scholarship, and entrenched narratives.

We continue our conversation:

Michael: I think you are right on in the framing of Tribalography for Indigenous scholar activism. I understand now, how absolutely blessed I was to begin my research journey under the instruction of the Salish-Pend d'Oreille Culture Committee (SPCC) and Elder Advisory Council (Elders). In doing so, I was taught, first-hand, appropriate ways to work with my community. Before my Elders would allow me to learn from and with them, my heart, values, and intention were assessed while numerous lessons were taught about values and appropriate ways of being. The entire process, intended to last a year, was completed in four. Atwen[3] consistently reminded me of the academic, scholarly, and anthropological work that had been done by researchers in the past who benefited first-hand and neglected to give anything back to our people.

Building relationships was the first step – with the Elders, with the Committee as a whole, the species we were learning about, and with each of the layers of experience that existed in those places. Each and every one of those places and beings now holds a very special place in my heart. We were respectful. We were responsible. And we reciprocated by returning a project, built by and with the Elders that was accurate, authentic, and appropriate for the children of our Sqelix[w4] communities.

It wasn't until I traveled to Arizona to begin my doctoral program that I learned of the research paradigms and methodologies of the dominant system. I began to question my ideas, my motives, and my intentions in doing research – the dominant research paradigms did not fit. Or maybe I do not fit easily within dominant ways of researching. In returning to my community, respecting the philosophies of my Elders, and learning of Wilson's (2008) 'cutting edge' work, I returned to my original path utilizing the Indigenous paradigm I was taught initially. As a person from Missoula who is Sqelixʷ and white, I am blessed to be slowly welcomed back into our Sqelixʷ tribal communities. As an Indian educator, I am trying to reclaim education, in a traditional sense, for the purpose of reclaiming our culture and strength as Sqelixʷ, and other Indigenous people.

> Lee: I like the way you reframe tribalography from your learnings, not only as centering the historical narratives, as Howe describes, but as the way in which knowledge is attained and transferred. I think we are often forced to consume the single, Western narrative and forget that there are other ways that are aligned to our communities and ways of knowing. I'm reminded of a time during the final semester of my doctoral courses. We had a required course for preparing our dissertation proposals. At the beginning of the course, I was intent upon seeing a new type of scholarship emerge. I didn't want to write the standard dissertation: five chapters – intro, lit review, methodology, data, analysis. I was seeking something authentic but I wasn't quite sure what that looked like. So it was a struggle to try and articulate how that could be researched. Our first assignment in the class was to develop a timeline/strategy for developing the proposal. I created a number of models in working with my advisor. But he kept asking me if this was an authentic representation of the work I wanted to accomplish. In other words, did the process match the research, the scholarship. That was the key.

I spent a few more days staring at what I first put together, the linear version, and then created a new version. It began with a circle. It was cyclical and based on the directions. It was the representation of an Indigenous timeline. It finally matched the process to the outcome. I think this is the exploration of tribalography, as you described. It moves beyond the story orientation to dig deeper to the process by which we transfer the stories.

> Michael: Yes, and that is especially important when faced with the hostility of higher education toward Indigenous realities; ways of knowing and ways of being.
>
> Lee: Right.

Survivance

> Columbus landed in the second grade for me, and my teacher made me swallow the names of the boats one by one until in the bathtub of my summer vacation I opened my mouth and they came back out-Nina, Pinta, Santa Maria-and bobbed on the surface of the water like toys. I clapped my hand over my mouth once, Indian style, then looked up, for my mother, so she could pull the plug, stop all this, but when I opened my mouth again it was just blood and blood and blood. (Jones, 2005, p. viii)

Survivance is a term that refers to the survival, endurance, and resistance of Indigenous people in the face of genocide, oppression and tragedy. It speaks of the 'narrative resistance that creates a sense of presence over absence, nihility and victimry' (Vizenor, 2008, p. 1). Too often, Indigenous peoples are portrayed as tragically and historically oppressed, conquered, and colonized. These images have been forced into the collective consciousness through a colonial narrative, which removes the agency of the People in favor of tragic victimry (Atalay, 2008). From this narrative, Indigenous people become 'passive receivers of colonial actions' (Atalay, 2008, p. 601); they are figures in the grand story of colonization. This is one of the aspects that tribalography seeks to resolve. However, the deeper micro-aggressions toward Indigenous people continue to persist in narrative and in action. The concept of survivance seeks to unsettle these dynamics by highlighting the agency and 'imaginative sovereignty' (Vizenor, Justice, 'Literature, Healing' 103) of a people who continue to 'actively [resist] repeated attempts of cultural, spiritual, and physical genocide and simultaneously had profound effects and influence upon colonial settler populations and governments' (Atalay, 2008, p. 601). Further, survivance is expressed through the stories of the lived experiences of struggle and determination, in order to appreciate the power and strength of those who continue to survive. As Lockard writes (2008) 'a survivance storyteller is one who has faced the wiindigo and lived to tell the tale or, rather who has told the tale and so lived' (p. 211).

We continue the conversation:

Lee: I think the hostility is often unintentional but points to the ways in which Western institutions were and are not inclined to move beyond a limited window. And those who do not conform or capitulate are outsiders; they are not allowed access. Because it is not a system that values the knowledge of our people as a whole and I think that its always a continuous tension, a conflict when you have activist scholars, or sovereign activist scholars that come in and say, 'well but this is the way we do it back home' and then it's like, 'well if you want to graduate you'll need to conform'. And this is the story that you've told and this is the story that I've heard from other scholars, and this is the story from the email I just got. You can either conform or you cannot be here … if you want to do that learning you can go back on the rez and do your elder stuff. But I think we are able to work from the inside. We are able to resist, as much as we can, and we survive in order to pass on the story to the next generation. We use our lived experience as a means of identifying what has been targeted *at* us rather than *with* us and then we work to deliberately shift that space. It's the long game for Indigenous people, as we are still here after five hundred years of genocide, we're still here.

Michael: Absolutely.

Lee: What I find interesting is the parallel of that dynamic, the conform or get out. It's, you know, Westerner scholars or researchers who come out to Indigenous communities, and especially scholars, always talk about the Indians and their elder knowledge and, 'oh, the wisdom of the elders and how important it is'. But once we say that we are going to use that as part of our knowledge base, well then it's not academically relevant. It's not robust. You can't rely on that. Which is interesting because we hear that on the one hand, *that* elder knowledge is sanctified but then with the other hand it's easily dismissed. This happened to me in a class during my final semester. It was no secret about my Indigenous heritage and we were in a class about educational politics. I was telling a story to my cohort about some issues that were taking place back home. They had a good deal of context about the issue, so I zoomed back and forth with my narrative. Very Native, very Indigenous storytelling. The web, you know?

So our guest instructor stopped me near the end with a snide comment about how they didn't understand what I was talking about and how my communication style was not going to cut it when addressing politicos and that she was very confused didn't gel to my style. I was shocked that for all the talk about inclusion and social justice our program espoused, here I was being berated for addressing my colleagues in an authentic manner. It was infuriating. And so I shut down. Refused to speak for the rest of the class and the time that our guest instructor was in attendance, save for being called on. It was difficult but I survived. I got through the class and I completed my dissertation and in the way of survivance, I am able to tell the tale so the next generation is more prepared.

Michael: Absolutely, absolutely. Just like I thank goodness for the Indigenous scholars who *have* written something down for us. Right? As we continue our research, we have to have that previous generation there so we can say, 'no, look they're published. Their scholarship is relevant.' It's still not held as relevant as dominant scholars and scholarship. It still faces skepticism, dismissal, and aggression, but at least I can say that. At least I can point to their work. Then the other thing that just constantly kills me, and I think we need to include this, is the importance of including story. But not just pieces of story, more story in its entirety. Like, chunks of the story that are valid. It's stated in a lot of the research that's come before us, but I was just told the other day, 'you can't … people who use block quotes', and this is almost quoted, 'people who use block quotes aren't able to synthesize what they're learning', right? And I was like, arghhh, no! It's like, I *can* synthesize what I'm learning more than anything. I am a doctoral student who teaches synthesis. I would not be here if I couldn't synthesize … the idea that it's *already* been synthesized. The point within those types of stories is that I'm including it because it's about community meaning making, it's not about, you know, me trying to boil down what they've said so that I can have a little quote and then … throw out all of *my* amazing knowledge. It's saying that, from my perspective, I'm honoring the wisdom of the people who have said that, that story.

Lee: There is often hostility toward our stories as a legitimate form of knowledge. I think that is why we, or I, at least, work so hard to promote stories and storytelling as more than an entertainment. It is how we pass on all the wisdom that has come before us. I think that is how we exist as activists, sovereign activists. And scholars.

Michael: Right, and scholars.

Giftings, questions, and medicine

In any of our work as Indigenous scholars, we are guided by the words of noted Cherokee philosopher and scholar Weaver (2007) who writes, 'ultimately, I must ask myself "How does our work help or support Native peoples in their struggles?" We must constantly interrogate ourselves with such questions, and the day we stop asking them is the day we are lost' (p. 243).

With this in mind, we do not seek for dialog to end with our conversations, in a closed system, but rather, be gifted out to other Indigenous scholars who may have been struggling with similar ideas, concepts or issues in their efforts. Further, we pose these questions as a way to continue toward actualizing a state of sovereign scholarship and the entrenchment of Tribalography and Survivance as means of establishing an Indigenous scholarship free from the confines of settler-colonialism.

- How can Indigenous Activist Scholars (IAS) contribute to decolonization or Indigenizing research methodologies?
- How can IAS contribute to youth agency self determination and national development?
- How can utilizing the stories of our elders within Indigenous scholarship contribute to Indigenous scholarship within local and global Indigenous communities?
- How can utilization of the Indigenous methodologies discussed here contribute to decreasing oppression of Indigenous scholarship within academy?

Finally, we must also take the time to reflect on the ways in which we have been gifted and give thanks to those who have assisted us in our journeys. Anpao Duta Flying Earth, a Sioux educator refers to this as the sources where we get our medicine. This medicine is important to name as it grounds our work and allows us to continue to serve as sovereign activists for our communities and Indigenous people. Our final conversation:

> Michael: The medicine I have gained from each of the supportive people in my life spur me forward at times like last night, when my dad told me providing encouragement is like providing encouragement for Sun to rise – even though it always will. He talked about how he feels like he and my mom give reminders that it's ok to rise, especially during stormy times. It is received from my beautiful mother, who listens as I talk through and make sense of my newly gained understandings and how they apply to the people we love and hold dear day in and day out.

The medicine that helps me make that next step comes when my auntie – who I look to as one of the strongest Sqelixʷ women I know, someone who has served our tribe, the nation, our state, and has returned to serve our tribe and families again – provides encouragement because our people need me to graduate. Our people need the work the Elders and community want to do that will help me complete this doctoral journey – the work that will ultimately benefit our children, their educations, and our tribe in the future. The medicine that helps me towards making that next step comes from my yayá?, when she reminds me how proud she is of me because education, in our own terms, is so very important if our tribal people and nation are going to continue to survive – if we are going to thrive for generations to come.

I am lémt to each who have been named, and to my ancestors, family, Elders, community members, mentors, students, colleagues, and all who have had such an amazing impact on my life, and to t̓úpye?, for all of the blessings he has brought.

> Lee: My medicine comes from my father, grandmother, and great-grandmother; my lineage to the Pueblo of Laguna. They remind me from the other side that I was and continue to be Hanu Kawaik'a – from the People of Laguna. This medicine is strong and it has defined my academic career. I chose to pursue my Ph.D. because of the way I saw my local school system destroyed at the hands of an outsider who did not have the best interests of the people in mind. Using a position of academic privilege, that outsider was able to unmake a system that had been created by and for the people. I felt that it was my responsibility to not allow that to happen again, and so I headed to Texas to get my final degree. And now I am home. Back in Laguna working on rebuilding the education system.

My medicine comes from the stories I was taught as a boy. The ones I have held on to for more than 30 years, the ones I teach my child. Those stories that remind me who I am and where I come from.

The stories of my grandparents and great-grandparents and great-great-grandparents who lived and survived. Who passed on their knowledge so I would be able to learn and grow and thrive. Dawa'eh.

Notes

1. In using the term Indigenous, we are aware of the complex nature of both the word and the concepts that are derived from it. We are deliberate in its use, however, as an evolving term to discuss those people who identify as Native American, Aboriginal, First Nations, etc. In our conversations, it will be noted that we often substitute the above categorizations for Indigenous, though our meaning aligns with the concept of those groups who have identified themselves as first peoples of a particular location (Stewart-Harawira, 2005).
2. A note on the dialogic aspects of this work: the conversation(s) held between the authors is woven throughout the sections of the document. The change in voice is indicated in each instance.
3. Atwen is Tony in the Sqelixʷ (Salish) language as the Sqelixʷ language does not contain the same letters and sounds as English.
4. Sqelixʷ can be used in three ways. The first, is the linguistic identification for the joint body of Salishan speaking people (the Seliš and Qlispé) who now reside primarily on The Flathead Reservation. Sqelixʷ is also a term used to refer to the Salish language. Finally, Sqelixʷ also refers to 'Indian people', in general, in the Sqelixʷ language.

Disclosure statement

No potential conflict of interest was reported by the authors.

References

Armstrong, J. (2000). A holistic education, teachings from the Dance House: "We cannot afford to lose one Native child". In M. K. P. Ah Nee-Benham & J. E. Cooper (Eds.), *Indigenous educational models for contemporary practice: In our mother's voice* (pp. 35–44). Mahwah, NJ: Lawrence Erlbaum.

Atalay, S. (2008). No sense of the struggle: Creating a context for survivance at NMAI. *American Indian Quarterly, 30*, 597–619.

Brayboy, B. M. J. (2006). Toward a tribal critical race theory in education. *The Urban Review, 37*, 425–446. doi: 10.1007/s11256-005-0018-y

Cajete, G. (1994). *Look to the mountain: An ecology of Indigenous education*. Durango, CO: Kivaki Press.

Forbes, J. (1980). The development of a native American intelligentsia and the creation of D–Q University. In H. Lutz (Ed.), *D–Q University: Native American self-determination in higher education* (pp. 75–85). Davis, CA: Tecumseh Center.

Forbes, J. (1998). Intellectual self-determination and sovereignty: Implications for native studies and for native intellectuals. *Wicazo Sa Review, 13*, 11–23.

Francis, L., III (2001, Fall). *The shadow knows: A native philosophical perspective on the light and dark side of the soul*. Albuquerque, NM: Native Realities Online.

Horan, E., & Kim, S. (2013). "Then one day we create something unexpected": Tribalography's decolonizing strategies in LeAnne Howe's Evidence of Red. *Studies in American Indian Literatures, 25*, 27–52.

Howe, L. (1999). Tribalography : The power of native stories. *Journal of Dramatic Theory and Criticism, XIV*, 117–125.

Jones, S. G. (2005). *Bleed into me: A book of stories*. Lincoln: University of Nebraska Press.

Kovach, M. (2005). Emerging from the margins: Indigenous methodologies. In L. Brown & S. Strega (Eds.), *Research as resistance: Critical, Indigenous, and anti-oppressive approaches* (pp. 19–36). Toronto: Canadian Scholars' Press/Women's Press.

Lockard, J. (2008). Facing the wiindigoo: Gerald Vizenor and Primo Levi. In G. Vizenor (Ed.), *Survivance: Narratives of native presence* (pp. 209–220). Lincoln: University of Nebraska Press.

Ortiz, S. J. (2002). *Out there somewhere*. Tucson: University of Arizona Press.

Russell, S. (2010). *Sequoyah rising: Problems in post-colonial tribal governance*. Durham, NC: Carolina Academic Press.

Silko, L. (1981). Language and literature from a Pueblo Indian perspective. In L. Fiedler (Ed.), *English literature: Opening up the canon* (pp. 54–72). Baltimore, MD: Johns Hopkins University Press.

Smith, L. T. (2011). *Decolonizing methodologies: Research and indigenous peoples* (2nd ed.). London: Zed Books.

Stewart-Harawira, M. (2005). *The new imperial order: Indigenous responses to globalization*. London/Wellington: Zed Press/Huia Publishers.

Vizenor, G. (1994). *Manifest manners: Post-Indian warriors of surivance*. Hanover, NH: University Press of New England.

Vizenor, G. (2008). Aesthetics of survivance: Literary theory and practice. In G. Vizenor (Ed.), *Survivance: Narratives of native presence* (pp. 1–13). Lincoln: University of Nebraska Press.

Weaver, J. (2007). More light than heat: The current state of native American studies. *The American Indian Quarterly, 31*, 233–255.

Wilson, S. (2008). *Research is ceremony: Indigenous research methods*. Black Point: Fernwood Publishing.

I am, I am becoming: how community engagement changed our learning, teaching, and leadership

Matthew Militello, Marjorie C. Ringler, Lawrence Hodgkins and Dawn Marie Hester

ABSTRACT

We explore the development of community-engaged scholars and practitioners through two distinct lenses: faculty who facilitate engaged learning processes and student-practitioners who are enacting these processes in their work. We use an auto-ethnographic technique, our own stories, to describe the will (motivation) and capacity (knowledge) gained through community engagement. More importantly, we provide vivid accounts of marked differences in our teaching, learning, and leadership. As a result, we have become activists in our craft as practitioners and scholars.

Introduction

We are products of traditional, formalized educational systems. These provided each of us with credentials and licenses for our professional practice. More importantly, we are co-learners with our communities. Our families, neighborhoods, and cultural affinity groups all have deep impacts on what has shaped us and who we ultimately become. As scholars and practitioners these community engaged learning opportunities and experiences have made a deep and meaningful impact on our teaching, learning, and leading.

In this article, we each tell stories of the people and experiences that shaped us in becoming burgeoning activist scholars and practitioners. Our first teachers were those who we lived and worked with. Their main pedagogy was storytelling. Stories from and of our elders helped us learn: history, culture, and literacy. Teaching and learning was a local endeavor. These lessons helped us understand that the community itself can be formal textbooks for learning.

For us community engagement combines the individual and organizational need for social networks and the desire for efficiency and improvement. This science of engagement is rooted in two important aspects: the local context and the work. To begin, there must be a fundamental shift from working *in* to working *with* communities. This shift involves honoring the wisdom of those who reside in the very communities one wants to improve. Healthy community engagement requires the focus on the gifts community members currently hold (Horton, Freire, Bell, Gaventa, & Peters, 1990; McKnight & Block, 2010). Guajardo, Guajardo, Janson, and Militello (2015) stated:

> We need to understand and honor the past. We also need to reveal truths in order to craft new narratives owned by and lived by the very people and places that need positive changes ... when people share their stories in public with those who have similar experiences from different communities, from different generations, or with different gifts, a collective and creative energy and focus take shape. (pp. 25, 146)

We also examine how our community-based teaching and learning manifests in our current practice. We embrace the pedagogies of community engagement through the ecologies of self, organization, and community (Guajardo et al., 2015) – these pedagogies define our work as activist scholars and practitioners. We begin with the ecology of self through individual stories that have shaped each of us. We unpack these stories in order to understand how the formal and informal educational structures foster or inhibit the important aspect of understanding self. Next we examine the ecology of the organization through our current practice. These practices – ways of knowing – help to understand how we have put our learning of self into our ways of doing. We conclude with a discussion around the implications of community engagement and community-engaged scholars. That is, we make the argument for a new canon of teaching and learning for school leaders.

Story by and as design

Biographies and autobiographies have provided rich data to document and analyze the development and power of engagement in the preparation of school and district educators (Ochs & Capps, 1996; Wolcott, 2003; Wortham, 2001). Similarly, our design is organic and rooted in the principles of understanding self and practice through stories. Our findings are illustrated through a series of autobiographical stories. Here, each author provides reflections and accounts of experiences that have shaped their work and learning. We wanted to take a storytelling perspective for this work. That is, together we, the authors, engaged in exercises to write, share, and reflect on our own stories.

We utilized an 'I Am' poem as a tool or pedagogy to elicit stories (Freeology, n.d.; Guajardo et al., 2015). These pedagogies are narrative methodologies that have proven beneficial to this work. Beginning with our own stories and then nesting these stories in our work to prepare and become prepared educational leaders was a powerful methodology.[1]

The authors of the *Abundant Community* stated that the 'primary function of a family, neighborhood, or community is to create its story. Telling the story gives body to the collective' (McKnight & Block, 2010, p. 95). We agree. The research methodology in this article was our own expressive form that was shaped by our own storytelling to one another. Guajardo and Guajardo (2013) dubbed this as Plática – 'Plática was performed in a language we understood, through an expressing cultural form that felt natural, and in a way that was respectful and affirming' (p. 162).

Ecology of self: the birth of community-engaged scholars

I am White.

~ Larry

The most powerful voice in my education was my Grandma Marie with Multiple Sclerosis.

~ Dawn

I'm an education engineer.

~ Marjorie

My teacher was an immigrant teaching migrants.

~ Matt

Larry: I am White

I am White. So were my parents. My father is from a small town in rural Maine with a population of less than 200. I remember witnessing the conversations in the general store, there was a strong sense of community and no apparent class boundaries but everyone was White. Growing up in the suburbs of New York City, I watched my dad develop a successful business based on the foundation of genuine relationships with people at all levels of his organization. Almost everyone was White.

I was groomed to understand that relationships were important. However, it was easy to develop relationships with people that looked like me because of shared common experiences. I have the perspective of a White, male. This perspective that was shared with others like me (ethnically and economically) was easy, but also restricting. I did not learn how restricting this perspective was until I began teaching at a minority–majority middle school in rural North Carolina at age 35.

I came to education after a brief career as a chemical engineer. My first teaching position was at an all-White private school near Boston. Seeking a place with a lower cost of living, I moved to North Carolina to teach at a mostly White charter school. When the charter school was not what I thought it was going to be, I interviewed for jobs at several schools. In every instance, 'do you think you can handle teaching minority students?' was the first question asked. I was stunned by the question and was not hired by multiple schools but did secure a middle school math position.

There was a time when I viewed the work by Ruby Payne as a kind of 'how-to' guide for working with disadvantaged students. It made logical sense to me that students have underperformed because of some (or many) deficiencies in their lives. Like most teachers, I was in the profession because I wanted to make a difference, but I found myself working with students that I did not understand. Acknowledging my Whiteness was an important step to understanding how my students (and their families) see me.

During my transition from all-White private school to majority Black public school, I became more aware of the educational inequities that exist along socioeconomic and racial lines. I also came to realize that it was an issue that I wanted to work on. As a White male I have easier access to traditional power structures than Black students and families. I have come to see my privilege as an 'asset' that I can use to bring about positive change.

Dawn: I am an author

I am an author. I was in the second grade when I wrote a book called *A Special Friend*. It told the story of a friendship between a boy named Joey and myself. He was my friend and was physically disabled. Although he was confined to a wheelchair and could not talk, he showed incredible courage. The protagonist of my first book did not win a medal at the Special Olympics but never complained.

This book is also a reflection of the strength of my grandmother. As long as I can remember my Grandma Marie was in a wheelchair and could not speak. She lived with multiple sclerosis (MS) for 50 years. Grandma Marie was born in Providence, RI on 30 April 1917. She was the oldest of a family of five children. Grandma Marie had a normal active childhood. This all changed when at the age of 17 her brother noticed her dragging her left leg while in line for communion. Over the next three years the intermittent dragging of her leg was somewhat ignored or was not considered to be significant. She married at age 22 and shortly after, her husband joined the Navy and served in WWII.

Grandma Marie gave birth to three sons and one daughter. It was in the mid-1950s that she was medically diagnosed with MS. Initially, Grandma Marie could walk by holding on to furniture, using a cane, and frequently leaning on her children's shoulders. She would walk for eleven blocks every Sunday so she could attend church. People thought she was drunk. She said nothing and kept her head high. All during this time Grandma Marie was never discouraged with her physical limitations and never complained about all the pain she was experiencing. She lost her ability to walk while her husband was fighting in the WWII. She continued to raise their four children. When my grandfather returned home she had lost most of the ability to speak. Even though she could not speak, my father often reminded me that she would always say that a perfect day is when you can do something for someone and they can never ever pay you back.

When we would go to her house, my sisters and I would get in bed with Grandma Marie, and talk to her, tell her stories, put makeup on her face and fix her hair. We would help Grandma Marie eat meals and help her dress in the morning. No one ever felt embarrassed when we would go out with her in her wheelchair shopping, out to eat, or to church, even though we saw the stares. She tried so hard to tell me her stories, but could not. I wanted so badly to hear her voice and the stories she wanted to share. I could see the stories of her life in her eyes. I knew at that very young age that I would be her voice.

Her courage, faith, and love were exemplified through me at a young age. Helping people with disabilities became a natural 'thing' for me. In third grade my sister and I would push the wheelchair of a fellow student with cerebral palsy and help him eat in the school cafeteria. He was Joey. All of this led me to write the book about Joey and wanting and needing to become a teacher. Now people say that this must be why I selected a career in Special Education. I say actually it selected me because there is more than one Joey and Grandma Marie in the world who needs a voice and advocates for them, verbally and nonverbally.

Marjorie: I am an education engineer

I am an education engineer. My earliest memories of school start with my third-grade teacher, Ms Overholser in my school in Colombia, South America. Ms Overholser made learning a collaborative occasion. I remember that our desks were organized in squares where I faced a friend and to my side I had two more friends. In groups we would tackle 'fun' yet rigorous projects and often we were expected to 'be the teacher' and teach others about our work. Ms Overholser also instilled in us a sense of civic duty. Our whole class sang as a choir during music. We sang mostly in English as Ms Overholser taught our subjects in English. Our choir would sometimes sing at nursing homes. The elders did not understand English, however, this did not matter; we saw smiles and dancing in our audience.

I graduated third in my class at an international school where all graduates were expected to attend college and choose careers such as engineering, medicine, or law. As expected I enrolled in an engineering program in the United States. I performed at average levels instead of at the top of my class. I had this nagging feeling that a career in engineering was not in my life's path and so I went to my advisor and asked, 'Do you see me as an engineer?' My advisor validated my concerns. It turned out that grades were a symptom of a bigger issue. I was used to learning cooperatively and working with classmates instead of competing against them. After this advising session I decided to explore different options and enrolled in 'Introduction to Education' – a life-changing decision – the best decision I ever made!

This introduction to education had me visiting schools and watching teachers in action. I saw students' express their 'aha' learning moments and this took me back to my high school years where I was at the top of my class and I enjoyed learning in study groups. Thinking back, there was a pattern with my study groups – I would pair up with friends that were not 'getting it' and I remember the feeling of accomplishment of watching them go through their own 'aha' learning moments. One particular friend, Soraya, was my biggest challenge. She simply was not able to grasp the content in class and I remember spending many afternoons at her house working through factoring problems with her. My patience had no limits. I was determined to help her learn math. These memories inspire me. Recently, I attended my 30-year high school reunion and many of my friends commented on how thankful they were that I helped them!

My elementary and secondary schooling experiences instilled in me the values of learning collaboratively, learning rigorous content, and engaging with my community to serve. It is important for me to afford similar types of opportunities to those I am in contact with. I did so by teaching high school students. I loved teaching yet as I looked outside my classroom too many high school students were not excited about learning as I thought they should be, and how I was. I decided to be a school administrator so that I could continue to teach in a larger context where my teachers were 'students' and my classroom would be the school building. At my large high school the teacher turnover rate was huge – we hired approximately 20 new teachers every year. Analyzing the turnover rate with the eyes of an education engineer, I felt that I could be a part of the solution if I entered higher education where educators are trained. Hence, I am now working in a principal preparation program as an education engineer to infuse the values instilled in me during my forming years: collaboration, high expectations for learning, and engaged scholarship. My job is to engineer principals that help nurture, support, and develop teachers that stay in the classrooms and love teaching.

My first semester teaching in higher education was trying. I was planning my lessons on a weekly basis barely staying ahead of my graduate students' readings. Because I was struggling I fell into the trap of creating power points summarizing assigned readings and did not include any learning opportunities. I lectured … and my graduate students were disappointed and uninterested. I had the same feelings of isolation that crept in when I was studying to be an engineer. I had to do something to make sure that my teaching resulted in preparing principals to do their jobs well. Like an engineer, I studied the problem and designed a solution. I did a lot of reading about instructional strategies and about engaging our community in learning. I started by changing my course assignments to include meaningful field experiences. At first I communicated with selected principals about the idea of my students engaging with them to complete projects that would contribute to the school's improvement efforts and at the same time be learning opportunities for my students. Next, I enlisted the help of another professor teaching the same course with another set of students. Together we outlined the field experience requirements and coached our students through a service learning project.

Engineering collaboration among faculty and school principals became a reality and students were sharing many exciting learning opportunities that in turn enriched the course discussions. My faculty partner and I shared the results with our colleagues and through many discussions decided to adopt service learning in seven of our nine courses! Now, five years later, the master of school administration program prepares servant leaders through service learning. I now understand that education is my vocation and engineering learning through community engagement is my passion.

Matt: learning love from an immigrant who taught migrants

I am the son of teachers. As the oldest of 10 in an Italian family from Detroit, my father, Ronald Angelo Militello, was sent to the seminary. After eight years he decided that he had a different calling. He put himself through school working the East-end Fruit Market in the late 1950s and early 60s. He eventually became the principal of the high school I attended. As a result, I was keenly aware of the formal educational structures. I had the 'inside baseball' information to navigate the traditional structures. However, it was the educational experiences that my mother provided that would instill the most discomfort and the most learning in my adolescence.

My mother dropped out of high school in the 10th grade. Living in Mexico City, my mother, Blanca Rosa Cárdenas, lived through the death of her mother at a very young age. My mother cared for her father while living at home. In 1967 she met my father while he vacationed in Mexico City with his teaching colleagues. By the end of that year they would be married and my mom would relocate to Michigan.

Coming to the United States with a limited proficiency in the English language was a challenge. The challenge became even greater when our family moved to a rural part of Michigan. My mother understood this challenge. She volunteered on a regular basis in Lena, Wisconsin, 40 miles from our home. Lena was home to a number of migrant farms. These migrant families would travel from South Texas each spring and work through the fall. The children of these families would enroll in the local schools in the middle of the second semester and leave midway through the following semester. The local schools were ill-equipped to work with mobile populations and especially challenged to work with second language learners.

During the summer, my mother would bring my brother and me to the migrant farms so she could work with the children. She taught English. The woman that would tell us to put the dirty dishes in the garage, the woman who spoke 'Spanglish,' on a good day, sought to provide the very basic language elements to the workers and their families.

My mother did not just 'teach English.' She engaged in pedagogies of relationships. Learning English may have been the formal objective, but it was the emotive needs that were being met. Looking back, she was not only fulfilling the needs of the migrant population, this immigrant herself was fulfilling her own needs. There was clearly an unspoken message of working with others – side-by-side. There were as many hugs and conversations and drives to navigate local services as there were formal English lessons.

It has been said that concepts like compassion and charity are synonymous with love. If her compassion and charity were merely a task or job to check off I would tend to agree. But love is more important than descriptions, elements, or manifestation of love. What I *witnessed*, what I *engaged* in as a child, what I *learned* was not compassion, nor charity. It was love itself. What I came to realize was the only profession that would allow me to actualize this love was education.

Making meaning of the stories of self

These four distinct stories tell about our individual paths to the profession of education. All four of us began this journey as classroom teachers. Marjorie and Matt later became faculty in educational leadership programs. Larry and Dawn moved into leadership positions in school districts. Our personal stories provide a context and background for our motivations. Since everybody has their own stories and motivations, it is important to start with deep self-reflection with peers. Our 'I am' poems were essential to dig deep and find our inner motivations.

The enterprise of understanding ourselves is difficult. This work is developmental, idiosyncratic, and highly contextualized. That is, understanding self takes place at different times for different people in a variety of settings. Place, space, style, personal beliefs, experiences, and interests all intersect simultaneously. What a person already knows, experienced, and likes deeply shapes one's worldview and ultimately their practice (Dewey, 1929).

How we know one another matters. Robert Putnam studied how there is a move from community toward individualism. Putnam (2000) tells the story of a friendship made through a bowling league that led to a person donating a kidney to another: 'that they bowled together made all the difference' (p. 28). Humans have a desire and need for relationships. Moreover, relationships are both cognitive and affective. Duncan-Andrade (2009) states, 'at the end of the day, effective teaching depends most heavily on one thing: deep and caring relationships' (p. 91).

The relationship web between the four of us is intricate. Dawn was drawn to getting her administration degree to continue to be the voice of Grandma Marie. Coincidentally, Dawn knew Marjorie through the local country club where Dawn worked to supplement her teacher income. There was a natural connection between Dawn and Marjorie because they both were in education and as Dawn pondered her decision of getting her master's degree Marjorie was there to help her think through her options. Similarly, Larry entered into his master's degree and met Matt, one of his professors. Larry and Matt connected through the community learning exchanges (CLEs) that were a part of their program of study. Matt joined the faculty at ECU and this is when his path crossed with Marjorie's. Dawn is now a graduate of the Educational Leadership department. Larry is now a doctoral candidate in the Educational Leadership department and both Matt and Marjorie are faculty in the same department.

Sociologist George Homans (1950) and colleagues spent years in Hawthorne Works outside of Chicago (a telephone equipment plant with 45,000 employees). A number of studies generated famous findings including the Hawthorne effect (a short-lived increase in workers efficiency by simple changes such as lighting). Homans' studies were focused on three elements of the workers:

- Activity (what people do),
- Interaction (relationships to one another), and
- Sentiment (internal feeling).

Homans found interdependency in this triumvirate. Actions and relationships matter most when it comes to one's sentiment. In turn, sentiment has the greatest impact on work (both efficiency and quality). Each of our individual stories has elements of activity, interaction, and sentiment. Each of us had mentors that created space for deep, meaningful conversation rooted in questions rather than answers, in practice rather than telling. Using Homan's theory of sentiment, activity, and interaction we derive the constant in our stories. Our common sentiment is that we are a part of our communities and that we learn with each other. Our common activity is education and our common interaction is the relationship we have forged through our community engagement.

Next we examine the ecology of the organization through our current practice. These practices – ways of knowing – help to understand how we have put our learning of self into our ways of doing.

Ecology of the organization: our practice

Teaching with community is a manifestation of love.

~ Matt

I have to own my Whiteness, I harness my privilege as a vehicle for the greater good.

~ Larry

Deep learning occurs through authentic experiences that benefit all parties involved.

~Marjorie

My role as a leader is intrinsically tied to my engagement with my community.

~Dawn

Matt: the blueberry teacher

My first teaching job was on the eastern shores of Lake Michigan. A small city that had the moniker of an 'All American City.' The city was known to be very conservative. Beneath the surface, often hidden, were large enclaves of rich, diverse cultures. One such group was known as the 'Blueberry Kids.' I was told that one of the greatest challenges in the district was teaching the migrant students who would start the school year and leave in the fall only to return in April. I had gotten to know this population well. They lived and worked on blueberry farms just outside of town. I soon discovered the apartments that were visible just off of US 31 were the exemption to the housing of migrant families. I took kids home after football practices – driving behind the apartments on a two-track dirt road. I understood why the farm owners and city council did not want people to know what the living conditions were really like.

The discovery of this did not make me feel sorry for students – who was I to put my values on their lives? Nor did I think they were receiving an inadequate upbringing from their families. What I discovered was their silencing by the educational system was a detriment to the learning. Why should I teach history with a textbook if I had primary historians in our district? Why should we discriminate the hard work of handpicking blueberries on a humid 95 degree day from a 9–5 air-conditioned office job? The fact remained the Blueberry Kids were treated differently. At times the discrimination was explicit, but mostly is was just normative practice – institutionalized with practices and policies.

Memories of the work I did with my mom at the migrant farms some 400 miles away came rushing back. I became a person many marginalized students could approach. At the end of my first year, I nominated a student for the local newspaper's student of the month award. I found myself having to advocate my case before a panel. I nominated a young migrant student who played basketball on my team. Danny was not an exemplary student by the usual metrics of report card grades. I was immediately taken to task on the main premise of my argument: Danny was the primary caregiver for his young siblings each day after school. I had to pursue a line of argument the committee was not often given, that this young man had adult responsibilities that he took seriously. He not only 'watched' his siblings, he taught his siblings, often asking me for activities he could lead with his brothers and sisters. My persuasion, if not persistence, paid off. Seeing his picture in the paper was satisfying, because it was disruptive – it honored a non-traditional face.

This disruptive force followed me into administration and now as a university professor. I have used my experiences and my work with colleagues around the country to advance the work of the CLE.[2] I work with students to understand that there is power in the place (context) and the wisdom of current community members. Moreover, we co-design experiences to understand the fundamental difference between *working for* and *working with* community members. For example, students experienced community walks and site visits where local community members shared stories of historical trauma and also ideas to improve their communities. These pedagogies were intergenerational and flipped the traditional power structure from the external educational experts and privileged the local elders and youth. Finally, I have been privileged to be able to support student attendance at CLEs around the country. There students were able to experience powerful learning, create national networks, and most importantly, operationalize their new ways of knowing into new ways of doing in their own work.

This work has infiltrated both the master and doctoral programs in the universities I have worked. The changes in the organization were manifested in love long ago by witnessing my mother's teaching and later engaging in that same teaching of love myself.

Larry: I live community engagement

I continue to reflect on my experiences and move forward as a leader. As a White male that has enjoyed a privileged life I have access and position to affect meaningful change. In February 2014, I organized a one-day CLE at my school to chart a new, more inclusive course for my school community. Students, parents, and community members interacted with board members, school administrators, and university professors to share their perspectives.

The most significant organizational challenge for me was to find the people who have real influence in the community and want to see positive change. It was difficult for me because I am White and not from rural eastern North Carolina. My key moment was speaking with one of the school custodians who in turn put me in touch with the pastor at a church where 1960s era civil rights protests were organized. The pastor invited me to attend church services and gave me an opportunity to address the congregation to explain the event I was organizing. Community members graciously allowed me to access a network of people that I otherwise never would have encountered.

White school leaders can continue to conduct business as usual in diverse communities but, based on my experience, we are in a unique position to bring people together. My White privilege and job status give me access to the traditional power structures and decision-makers. The authentic relationships I have built with students, families, and school staff that are based on trust have enabled me to become part of a community that does not look like me but with whom I share common values. It is then my responsibility to bring the White and non-White communities together for healing and to work on problems that we all face. The CLE is ideally suited for this task because it demands that participants simultaneously have their own voice and learn from others.

One year after my CLE, a bus driver who attended was inspired to take action to resolve a long-standing feud between two students. She gathered the students and families at a local church. With the help of a pastor, she spent more than an hour giving everyone the opportunity to share their side of the story.

In recounting her story, she said this was the first time she felt a school really cared about all of its students in 40 years. She took action because she felt confident that her efforts would be reinforced and supported by the school leaders. We recorded our conversation about the impact of her experience with the CLE and my larger efforts to build a more inclusive school community. The following is a link to a few excerpts from that discussion: http://vimeo.com/edutrope/larrycle.

My CLE experiences were the basis for a fundamental shift in my worldview. I now view my students with an asset model in mind. I ask myself, what attributes am I seeing that I can guide students to develop? How can I empower these talented young people to take ownership of their future? It is, after all their future – not mine.

The Northeast Leadership Academy at North Carolina State University prepared me to become a community-based school leader. As part of my master's program, Dr Matt, introduced me to the CLE and the work of Myles Horton. I was intrigued by Myles Horton's conviction that the power and wisdom of local people could be used to solve most challenging problems. Horton's philosophies influenced my thoughts about my role as a school leader and the possibilities for empowering my students and community.

I learned how the power of place and the wisdom of people could be combined to create powerful and inspiring learning experiences that not only honored our past but created possibilities for the future. With experience, I began to understand that a CLE is not only a carefully sequenced series of pedagogies but also a paradigm through which I now view leadership. My mindset shifted from a traditional hierarchical view of leadership to one that is inclusive. I now seek opportunities for distributive leadership and value community input in my school.

Marjorie: I lead a master of school administration with community engagement

I am a professor that believes that deep learning occurs through authentic experiences and these experiences benefit all parties involved. Authentic learning experiences in principal preparation are achieved by working side by side with effective principals, teachers, and school stakeholders to engage in meaningful projects in schools. Service learning is a great vehicle to do so. Through dialog and research studies our faculty became convinced that service learning could be implemented, studied, and used as the basis for national accreditation. My role has been to keep the dialog and studies at the forefront. I schedule our monthly meetings, develop the agenda, and push for engagement, while facilitating our ongoing program improvement studies.

As a team, our faculty, meets on a monthly basis to study our student learning, review data, and make pedagogical decisions to improve principal preparation. We focus on ways to experientially weave content and practice changing the role of faculty to facilitators and coaches of learning. We redesigned our program of study to develop leaders that engage with their community through reflective problem solving, culturally competent communication, integrity, service-minded collaboration, and innovative strategies. These processes take commitment and I became the advocate that fostered and nurtured our team's resolve.

We labeled our principal preparation authentic learning experiences as *Service Leadership Projects* (SLPs). We derived SLPs from servant leadership (Greenleaf, 1990) and service learning (Bringle, Hatcher, & McIntosh, 2006). To us a servant leader listens and empathizes with his/her followers and helps each individual reach their personal potential while developing his/her self. We wanted to prepare servant leaders and we did so by adopting service learning as our pedagogy. Now, when we recruit students and collaborate with principals to help us prepare future leaders we explicitly discuss our philosophy and caringly market this as an equation: *Servant Leadership + Service Learning = Service Leadership.*

Engaging with our practicing principals to collaboratively prepare our future leaders was not difficult. On the contrary, our practicing principals welcomed the idea and now have lists of meaningful projects ready for our students. The challenge has been convincing our higher education institution that engaged scholarship is a form of research. Our dean and graduate faculty did not see the value of engaged scholarship and blocked our work because it did not fit the mold of traditional research. We were told that we were not able to study effects and compare them to 'control' groups or to conduct purely quantitative studies to determine significance. However, our local school principals were noticing changes in their schools and facilitating authentic learning experiences for our students. By now I was convinced that part of my job was to actively push back the traditional ivory tower thinking about scholarship. I now had stories to show off the impact of the SLPs. Our students created digital stories of the work they were accomplishing and these stories were powerful proof of impact.

I capitalize on every chance that I have to share the SLPs with my students, colleagues, my supervisors, and our stakeholders. I use digital stories to share benefits and challenges. Each project that students engaged in at a school has become a powerful story of learning to be a leader. Our students are making a difference. Joshua, one of our students, engaged in a project to work with a rural high school community to increase awareness of the college opportunities available to high school graduates. In the process of shaping the project, Joshua talked with administrators, teachers, parents, and students to get a picture of students' knowledge about college opportunities. Joshua was appalled to find out that in his rural high school students were not aware of many opportunities and that the majority of students only started asking these questions their senior year. His project involved organizing a college awareness week at the school. He invited ninth graders to this event. In planning this event Joshua and I discussed many things and I asked if he would consider bringing these high school students to our university campus. He had not thought about this option. I gladly connected him with the director of undergraduate admissions and they scheduled an on campus visit for his high school students. The impact of this project was huge for all. Joshua's digital story may be seen at this link: https://www.youtube.com/watch?v=mmL4BqwC1y8. The Master of School Administration (MSA) program's SLP YouTube channel with other digital stories may be viewed at this link: https://www.youtube.com/channel/UCO50oR28UW__uyfzG4odHyg.

Dawn: I live community engagement in my master program

My first SLP instigated a two-year restructuring process of our literacy program due to the large amount of readers reading below grade level and the need to comply with the North Carolina Read to Achieve Program as part of the Excellent Public Schools Act.

The next five SLPs revolved around and were an extension of how to improve our literacy needs. I expanded this first SLP experience with purposeful and powerful professional learning communities, increased parent involvement through open table talks at literacy open house events, increased recognition and celebrations of student and educator achievement, and empowered staff by working collaboratively. The last SLP infused character education and cultural diversity into our already existing English Language Arts curriculum. Collectively, these SLPs changed the lens in which I view my school and the way in which I lead.

It was the last semester before I completed the MSA at East Carolina University. My pedagogical philosophies were strengthened through the SLPs by understanding that my role as a leader was intrinsically tied to my engagement with my community. My path crossed again with Matt, Marjorie, and Larry when we traveled to Texas to participate in the North Dakota Study Groups (NDSG) at the Llano Grande Center in Edcouch, Texas. At NDSG we explored *Historias de Educación: Pedagogy, Language, and Social Change*. I was a bit overwhelmed being surrounded by so many strong activists. I heard everybody speak about the power of stories and the power of community engagement. The experience guided me to be vested in and understand the power of a CLE. I came back to North Carolina with a new infused curiosity about my own school's heritage and history. Matt, Marjorie, and I began working collaboratively to create a first time CLE as part of my final SLP of my master program. We would tell the story of one of the oldest schools in our community.

I work at an educational center that I discovered has a rich history that no one ever spoke about. This school was originally built in 1903. It has been known by numerous names: the Greenville Industrial High School, the Greenville Graded School, the Fifth Street or the Fleming Street School, and now Sadie Saulter Educational Center after one of the principals. The school building was the first Greenville Graded School for Black students and it remained there until the school burned down in 1970. The students then went to a White high school and this accelerated desegregation in our community. I found myself cold calling elders of the community as I was gathering more and more information. A few weeks later I was sitting in the living room of an elder named Jimmye and his buddy Ernest. They shared the stories of the community and the story of the schools. They were the voice of the past.

This experience has molded me as I begin my role as an educational leader. There is a need to hear these voices and continue to pass on this history of our community in our schools. It is what has shaped us for today. I know that I need to engage with the community to do this job. I need to hear the voices of the community and be the voice to share these stories so they are not lost. Here is a link to my interview with Jimmye: http://vimeo.com/edutrope/jimmye.

Through SLP my leadership lens has become deeper and more dynamic. The SLPs that I completed in my MSA program have challenged me and molded my pedagogical approach and methodology. Within the SLPs I began to learn more about the historical cultures of my community. I began to talk to community members and hear their voices and stories that have shaped our schools today. I now infuse a collective aspect of community through oral history and academic activism in my pedagogy.

Making meaning of the organizational stories of practice

Research about adult learners in graduate education and their development of new epistemologies (knowledge of content), ontologies (identification with content knowledge), and practice (knowledge in use) indicates that the experience should not be contrived or didactic. Rather how students are taught must naturally blend with the content (Metz, 2001; Walker, 1999). Specific studies have focused on specific program designs such as cohort models (Barnett, Basom, Yerkes, & Norris, 2000), problem-based learning (Copland, 2000; Darling-Hammond, Meyerson, LaPointe, & Orr, 2010), and internships (Cordeiro

& Sloan, 1996; Ellis, 2002). However, a shift in epistemology requires more. It requires experiential learning (Schoenfeld, 1999), public learning (Schoenfeld, 1999), as well as peer-to-peer and student-to-faculty relationships (Austin, 2002).

Field practices were meant to integrate coursework and provide opportunities to practice leadership; however, it is often regulated to a simple accounting of internship hours. These experiences fail to provide candidates with opportunities to develop strong skills to work effectively with families and community (Miller, Lines, Sullivan, & Hermanutz, 2013). Studies suggest engaging parents, families, and communities can lead to positive student outcomes (Epstein, 2013; Fan & Chen, 2001; Goodall & Vorhaus, 2011; Henderson & Mapp, 2002; Jeynes, 2012). Khalifa (2012) argues that leading *in* the community, as well as in the school, constitutes a key practice of successful school leaders.

Higher education institutions have engaged with their communities sporadically. It is not a systemic requirement of universities because faculty's work is valued first by the research they publish, second by their teaching, and a distant third is their service to the community. The Carnegie Commission of Higher Education who developed, the Carnegie Classification to classify colleges and universities to support their programs and research institutionalizes this emphasis. In 1995, however, Ernest Boyer, President of the Carnegie Foundation for the Advancement of Teaching, presented a speech that created the Scholarship of Engagement. His speech criticized universities for sacrificing the scholarship of service and focusing mostly on research and teaching. This shift in scholarship distanced universities from 'addressing the nation's most pressing civic, social, economic, and moral problems' (p. 23). The scholarship of engagement, according to Boyer, should create 'a special climate in which the academic and civic cultures communicate more continuously and more creatively with each other to enlarge and enrich quality of life for all of us' (p. 33).

Matt and Marjorie, professors, provide an account of how they profess and model the construction of social capital in their students. There is praxis – merging theory and practice – that is clear in the form and function of the graduate education highlighted in this article. There is a belief and there is action that 'social capital … strengthens our better, more expansive selves. The performance of our democratic institutions depends in measureable ways upon social capital' (Putnam, 2000, p. 349).

Dawn's story of the evolution of her SLPs in a two-year time span illustrated how students in this program learn to lead and become civic minded in their professions. The revisioned principal preparation program capitalizes on every experience to serve as an opportunity to learn thus facilitating community engagement. This philosophy permeates instruction in the program.

Larry's story of living community engagement is inspiring. Larry has broken through stereotypes and reached the heart of educational matters through caring. He engages because he cares. The community members he interacts with can feel his sincerity and his ability as a leader. Larry also feels the sincerity of the community members and senses the power they have within their community. Larry's caring is deeper because he is engaged in critical self-analysis focused on his whiteness, on his cultural self, and on his teaching. Larry's story significantly contributes to leadership development through his particular kind of caring. Larry inserts the realities of White privilege and examples of how to use it to show love. He acknowledges and then acts on his privilege.

Implications of community engagement and community-engaged scholars

Our organic stories rooted in the principles of understanding self and practice were illustrated through accounts of experiences that have shaped our work and learning. We conclude with a discussion around the implications of community engagement and community-engaged scholars. That is, we make the argument for a canon of teaching and learning for school leaders.

Developing a new epistemology and a new way of doing is difficult. In graduate education this is an acute challenge. Adult learners come with years of acquired knowledge through formal and informal education as well as personal interests and experiences. Our challenge as educators is to create new opportunities for learning. For us, this begins with self. There is an importance to understanding yourself before advancing new knowledge or an understanding of others. Our programs begin with such an examination. This is often therapeutic for learners.

Neumann, Pallas, and Peterson (1999) stated, 'In graduate school, a doctoral student may experience perhaps for the first time, an epistemological confrontation' (p. 259). This confrontation entails leaving behind a personal, particular, experiential, and normative cultural understanding for one that is analytical, intellectual, universal, and theoretical (Labaree, 2003). The four of us engaged in an epistemological confrontation. This confrontation was guided by opportunities we were each afforded. These often collided with our own prior learning and experiences. However, there is a clear sense that early on each of us had ingrained in us a sense of relationship and purpose to work with others.

Nonetheless, each of us had opportunities to engage 'in social practice where learning is the integral constituent' (Lave & Wenger, 1991, p. 35). Moreover, our learning was generative, contextualized, and space was granted for reflection. Argyris and Schon (1996) dubbed this as a double-loop learning process. Reflection without impact on practice is linear, whereas the process of reflection impacting one's action constitutes a generative, double-loop process.

Research has indicated that faculty assists graduate students in developing identity (Austin, 2002; Weidman, Twale, & Stein, 2001). Professors wield a great deal of power vis-à-vis what readings and assignments they assign as well as the manner in which they teach. Students in graduate education become a part of an educational/family tree of knowledge. That is to say, by who and how one is taught determine one's educational ancestry. In each case the authors have named specific educators throughout their lives. Interestingly, many were not their formal educators in the past.

In the case of the revisioned principal preparation program, the service leadership framework shattered traditional practices of lectures about leadership theory and broke the constraints of only learning from texts and from simulated learning activities contained in the physical space of college classrooms. The revisioned principal preparation program integrated learning in real situations alongside administrators, teachers, parents, students, and community members from the get go. Students in their first semester are challenged to understand themselves and to reflect on their leadership skills. After an intense analysis of themselves and reflecting on their findings, students then are provided many opportunities to continue reflecting as they learn the role of the principal. Dawn's story of the evolution of her SLPs in a two-year time span illustrated how students in this program learn to lead and become civic minded in their professions. Dawn believes that 'You earn a living by what you get, but more importantly, you live a life by what you give.'

Larry has developed a relationship of caring with his community and together they have engaged in positive relationships for a greater good. Like Larry, each doctoral student in the program has learned from Matt ethnographic techniques and community engagement pedagogies that promote positive change in schools.

As faculty who helped design both of these programs, our engaged scholarship centers on research about community engagement as an effective means to preparing principals and educational leaders. We write about pedagogies that engage communities in proactive collaborations and advocate for a reinvention of higher education based on the powerful effects of learning that our students share through their stories. We use an auto-ethnographic technique, our own stories, to examine the will (motivation) and capacity (knowledge) gained through community engagement. More importantly, we provide vivid accounts of marked differences in our teaching, learning, and leadership. As a result, we have become activists in our craft – practitioners and scholars.

Conclusion

Our communities are our texts.

Struggles can manifest into different ways of thinking and ultimately different ways of doing. This is true of individuals, organizations, and communities. In this article, we examined the ecology of self. The struggles of identification and of traditional processes each of us reflected upon helped us understand

and engage in different ways of knowing and doing. In turn, the organizations we work in were altered. Ultimately, the larger communities in which we live and work become partners – authentic partners, bridging the gap between the 'expert' at the university and the 'expert' in the community.

To be sure there are many benefits to global and formal teaching and learning including: *access to knowledge* (e.g. State Compulsory Education Laws (earliest in Massachusetts, 1852 and the last in Mississippi, 1917; *Brown v Board of Education*, 1954), *scientific investigation* (e.g. Newton's laws of physics and Einstein's theory of relativity), and *exploration* (e.g. Copernicus proving the sun was center of the universe and Magellan's first circumnavigation of the Earth) to name a few. However, there are other, non-canonical, learning opportunities often over looked even if more potent.

It is our hope that this auto-ethnographic examination of teaching and learning about community engagement leads to a new normative practice, an accommodation of knowledge for the next generation of educators. It is our strong belief that this leads to community engagement that respects and honors the local context and wisdom of elders and youth, presses for an asset-based approach rather than a constant focus on deficits, and ultimately leads to highly functional partnerships among schools, students, families, and communities.

Moore (2013) argues that situated learning will remain at the margins until faculty in higher education can embrace new practices. If we want to advocate for an inclusive, democratic society, then we as faculty must model it (Apple & Beane, 2007). It is difficult to study effects and compare them to 'control' groups or to conduct purely quantitative studies to determine significance. However, in the case of two professors of Educational Leadership, engaged scholarship has become the way to prepare school leaders to make a noticeable difference in schools. By working with faculty, graduate students, and schools' communities, school principals and superintendents are noticing the positive effects of engaging community members as a part of the school's improvement efforts.

As engaged scholars, we want to re-imagine the lessons of teaching and learning that are community based. This is difficult for both university faculty and students. University faculty and administrators do not see the value of engaged scholarship as a form of research and teaching. Engaged scholarship does not fit the traditional role of a university professor. We want to challenge our field. We want to move away from service learning – which is laudable, but unidirectional and incomplete – toward engaged learning – which highlights the deeper, generative, honoring experiences – our students need.

This work is not easy. Beyond the barriers of one's own learning, there are institutional barriers in the academy that must be overcome. Too often engaged scholarship is not accepted as a scholarly form of research. Thanks to the elective Carnegie Classification there is an option to engage in community-engaged scholarship (Noel & Earwicker, 2014); however, the institutionalization of empirical research as the most valued indicator of faculty work continues to discourage engaged scholarship. Few tenure and promotion committees have formal written guidelines for what consittutes community-engaged scholarship or accept this form of scholarship as part of academic promotion (Foster, 2010).

In this article, we strike at community engagement with the triumvirate of *know-why* (the philosophical premise of why this work is valuable), *know-how* (the procedural elements of how the work is done), and *doing* (the implementation of this work with fidelity and measures). In essence, we have created a logic model for community engagement for the activist scholar. The implementation of the model will take individual courage, it will challenge the organization, and it will provoke the institution of higher education. Courage, challenge, and provocation – important lessons teachers can pass along to their students.

Notes

1. Narratives have been used as a methodology and have proven valuable when one's own experience is the unit of analysis. The narratives became a tool that helped us to focus and reflect on the student experience (Abbey et al., 1997; Bruner, 1988; Chase, 2005; Denzin, 1994; Polkinghorne, 1988). In essence, the narratives helped us 'recall … strong metaphors, vivid characters, unusual phrasings, and the hold back on interpretation [which] invite the reader to emotionally "relive" the events of the author' (Sparks, 1988, p. 1).

2. A Community Learning Exchange is a gathering of community members focused on both assets the community possesses as well as issues that need attention. Members are inclusive of people from different viewpoints and agendas as well as a mix of youth and elders. The Community Learning Exchange was born out of a W.K. Kellogg Foundation national initiative called the Kellogg Leadership for Community Change (KLCC). Started in 2002, the goal of KLCC was to redefine leadership development to be more inclusive of a broad spectrum of the community (Benham, Militello, Elissetche, Oliver, & Ortiz, 2007; Benham, Militello, & Halladay, 2005). Working in 11 communities across the country, KLCC generated local and national networks of like-minded people focused on community development efforts. The CLE applies specific strategies or pedagogies that honor local context and people (Guajardo et al., 2015). Since 2008 more than 15 national CLEs have taken place. Additionally, numerous local CLEs have been implemented based on the national model.

Disclosure statement

No potential conflict of interest was reported by the authors.

References

Abbey, S., Bailey, B., Dubrick, J., Moore, K., Nyhof-Young, J., Pedretti, E., & Saranchuk, R. (1997). Multiparadigm voices of doctoral students: Shifting the boundaries of learning through a collaborative study process. *Qualitative Studies in Education, 10*, 101–115.

Apple, M. W., & Beane, J. A. (2007). *Democratic schools: Lessons in powerful education*. Portsmouth, NH: Heinemann.

Argyris, C., & Schon, D. (1996). *Organizational learning*. Reading, MA: Addison Wesley.

Austin, A. E. (2002). Preparing the next generation of faculty: Graduate school as socialization to the academic career. *The Journal of Higher Education, 73*, 94–122.

Barnett, B. G., Basom, M. R., Yerkes, D. M., & Norris, C. J. (2000). Cohorts in educational leadership preparation programs: Benefits, difficulties, and the potential for developing school leaders. *Educational Administration Quarterly, 36*, 255–282.

Benham, M., Militello, M., Elissetche, C., Oliver, J., & Ortiz, A. (2007). *Kellogg leadership for community change I longitudinal report*. Battle Creek, MI: W.K. Kellogg Foundation.

Benham, M., Militello, M., & Halladay, P. (2005). *Kellogg leadership for community change: Focus on teaching and learning. Final evaluation*. Battle Creek, MI: The W.K. Kellogg Foundation.

Boyer, E. L. (1995, October 11). *The scholarship of engagement*. Mechanicsburg, PA: The Ernest L. Boyer Center, Messiah College. Unpublished manuscript.

Bringle, R., Hatcher, J., & McIntosh, R. (2006). Analyzing Morton's typology of service pardignms and integrity. *Michigan Journal of Community Service Learning, 13*, 5–15.

Bruner, J. (1988). Life as narrative. *Language Arts, 65*, 574–583.

Chase, S. E. (2005). Narrative inquiry: Multiple lenses, approaches, voices. In N. K. Denzin & Y. Lincoln (Eds.), *The Sage handbook of qualitative research* (3rd ed., pp. 651–680). Thousand Oaks, CA: Sage.

Copland, M. A. (2000). Problem-based learning and prospective principals' problem-framing ability. *Educational Administration Quarterly, 36*, 585–607.

Cordeiro, P., & Sloan, E. S. (1996). Administrative interns as legitimate participants in the community of practice. *Journal of School Leadership, 6*, 4–29.

Darling-Hammond, L., Meyerson, D., LaPointe, M., & Orr, M. (2010). *Preparing principals for a changing world: Lessons from effective school leadership programs*. San Francisco, CA: Wiley.

Denzin, N. K. (1994). The art and politics of interpretation. In N. K. Denzin & Y. Lincoln (Eds.), *Handbook of qualitative research* (pp. 500–515). Thousand Oaks, CA: Sage.

Dewey, J. (1929). *Of a science of education*. New York, NY: Horace Liveright.

Duncan-Andrade, J. (2009). Note to educators: Hope required when growing roses in concrete. *Harvard Educational Review, 79*, 181–194.

Ellis, J. C. (2002). *A study of the internship component of the innovative leadership program at the University of Alabama from 1994 to 2000* (Unpublished doctoral dissertation). The University of Alabama, Tuscaloosa.

Epstein, J. (2013). Ready or not? Preparing future educators for school, family, and community partnerships. *Teaching Education, 24*, 115–118. doi:10.1080/10476210.2013.786887

Fan, X., & Chen, M. (2001). Parental involvement and students' academic achievement: A meta-analysis. *Educational Psychology Review, 13*(1), 1–22. doi:10.1023/A:1009048817385

Foster, K. M. (2010). Taking a stand: Community-engaged scholarship on the tenure track. *Journal of Community Engagement and Scholarship, 3*, 20–30.

Freeology (n.d.). *I am poem* [Web page]. Retreived from http://freeology.com/worksheet-creator/poetry/i-am-poem

Goodall, J., & Vorhaus, J. (2011). *Review of best practice in parental engagement*. London: Department of Education.

Greenleaf, R. (1990). *The servant as leader*. Indianapolis, IN: Tobert Greenleaf Center for Servant Leadership.

Guajardo, F., & Guajardo, M. (2013). The power of plática. *Reflections: Public Rhetoric, Civic Writing and Service Learning, 13*, 159–164.

Guajardo, M., Guajardo, F., Janson, C., & Militello, M. (2015). *Reframing community partnerships in education: Uniting the power of place and wisdom of people*. New York, NY: Routledge.

Henderson, A. T., & Mapp, K. L. (2002). *A new wave of evidence: The impact of school, family, and community connections on student achievement*. Austin, TX: Southwest Educational Development Laboratory.

Homans, G. (1950). *The human group*. New York, NY: Harcourt, Brace.

Horton, M., Freire, P., Bell, B., Gaventa, J., & Peters, J. (1990). *We make the road by walking: Conversations on education and social change*. Philadelphia, PA: Temple University Press.

Jeynes, W. (2012). A Meta-analysis of the efficacy of different types of parental involvement programs for urban students. *Urban Education, 47*, 706–742.

Khalifa, M. (2012). A re-new-ed paradigm in successful urban school leadership: Principal as community leader. *Educational Administration Quarterly, 48*, 424–467. doi:10.1177/0013161X11432922

Labaree, D. (2003). The peculiar problems of preparing educational researchers. *Educational Researcher, 32*, 13–22.

Lave, J., & Wenger, E. (1991). *Situated learning: Legitimate peripheral participation*. Cambridge, MA: Cambridge University Press.

McKnight, J., & Block, P. (2010). *The abundant community: Awakening the power of families and neighborhoods*. San Francisco, CA: Berrett-Koehler.

Metz, M. H. (2001). Intellectual border crossing in graduate education: A report from the field. *Educational Researcher, 30*, 12–18.

Miller, G. E., Lines, C., Sullivan, E., & Hermanutz, K. (2013). Preparing educators to partner with families. *Teaching Education, 24*, 150–163. doi:10.1080/10476210.2013.786889

Moore, D. T. (2013). *Engaged learning in the academy: Challenges and possibilities*. London: Palgrave Macmillan.

Neumann, A., Pallas, A. M., & Peterson, P. L. (1999). Preparing educational practitioners to practice educational research. In E. C. Lagemann & L. S. Shulman (Eds.), *Issues in education research: Problems and possibilities* (pp. 247–288). San Francisco, CA: Jossey-Bass.

Noel, J., & Earwicker, D. (2014). *Gathering data and documenting impact: 2010 Carnegie community engagement classificatoin application approaches and outcomes* (Working paper, 2014 Series, Issue No. 1). Boston, MA: New England Resource Center for Higher Education.

Ochs, E., & Capps, L. (1996). Narrating the self. *Annual Review of Anthropology, 25*, 19–43.

Polkinghorne, D. (1988). *Narrative knowing and the human science*. New York: State University of New York Press.

Putnam, R. D. (2000). *Bowling alone: The collapse and revival of American community*. New York, NY: Touchstone.

Schoenfeld, A. H. (1999). The core, the canon, and the development of research skills. In E. C. Lagemann & L. S. Shulman (Eds.), *Issues in education research: Problems and possibilities* (pp. 166–202). San Francisco, CA: Jossey-Bass.

Sparks, A. (1988). Narratives of self as an occasional conspiracy. *Sociology of Sport Online*. Retrieved from http://physed.otago.ac.nz/sosol/v1i1/v1i1a3.htm

Walker, V. S. (1999). Culture and commitment: Challenges for the future training of education researchers. In E. C. Lagemann & L. S. Shulman (Eds.), *Issues in education research: Problems and possibilities* (pp. 224–244). San Francisco, CA: Jossey-Bass.

Weidman, J. C., Twale, D. J., & Stein, E. L. (2001). Socialization of graduate and professional students in higher education: A perilous passage? *ASHE Higher Education Report, 28*(3), 1–112.

Wolcott, H. (2003). *The man in the principal's office: An ethnography*. Lanham, MD: Rowman Altamira.

Wortham, S. (2001). *Narratives in action*. New York, NY: Teachers College Press.

Skipping toward seniority: one queer scholar's romp through the weeds of academe*

Catherine A. Lugg

ABSTRACT

This reflective essay, which is both autobiographical and historical in nature, is framed by answering the questions posed by the editors regarding my work: What values inform it, how I actually do it, and why do I do it? Quite simply, I am writing to encourage social change for all queer people, be it merely the little corner of my own social world. Furthermore, I consciously strive to be a 'paid pestering queer.'

Queer studies offer us one method for imagining, not some fantasy of an elsewhere, but existing alternatives to hegemonic systems. (Halberstam 2011, Kindle Locations 1246–1247).

In 2015, I realized that somehow, to my great chagrin, I had become one of the 'old guys' of my field. Given my Ph.D. graduation date was in May of 1995, I am neither new, nor particularly 'hip,' and I'm definitely not a hipster in any sense of the term. So I have reconciled myself, somewhat, to the change in my professional status. What has become a bit more startling is that queer work is moving in from the margins of what is considered 'mainstream' research (if but a tiny bit) to at least make a showing at educational research conventions. While it still has a definite outsider cast – particularly in education – I am heartened by how far the work has come from the early 1990s. That said, there are endless lifetimes of research to be conducted in the fields of education, especially in the areas of educational administration and policy.

My own work flows from a combination of life experiences – both in and out of school – as well as my own reading of history, law, and more generally the social sciences and the humanities. Methodologically, I was trained as an historian of education. But given my grounding in queer theory and subsequent readings in law, I am not your mother's, or father's for that matter, historian. This reflective essay, which is both autobiographical and historical in nature, is framed by answering the following questions posed by the editors:

- What is your work and what values inform it?
- How do you do this work?
- Why do you do this work, i.e. to what end?

I suspect some of the readers will be disconcerted by my observations and experiences, but to some extent, that is precisely the point. If you are going to engage advocating for social justice issues as part of your larger research, teaching and service agendas, you must become what Michael Eric Dyson calls, 'a paid pest.' You must embrace the inevitable failures that will accrue as you engage with those with white skin privilege, who own a chromosomal penis, who blather on about the glories of heterosexual

---

*With apologies to Dan Savage, who has a book (2002) with somewhat the same title (substitute 'Gomorrah' for 'Seniority'). Savage's book was comedic and very queer response to conservative legal scholar Robert Bork's 1996 book, *Slouching towards Gomorrah*.

lust, love, and sex, while sporting the perfect and perfectly white teeth of the upper middle class. Those of us who are professors, particularly those of us at major research institutions, have enormous class privileges – including that we can get our teeth fixed. These are then compounded if we are white, and/or male, etc. (see Hutchinson, 1997; Valdes, 1995). Finally, unlike the vast majority of Americans, we can control the nature of our labor, at least somewhat, and if we are ferociously persistent, we can see the fruits, or in my case, the fruity fruits or our labor.

In the beginning…

We're here!! We're Queer!!! GET OVER IT!!! (Queer pride chant from the early 1990s).

My work has been clearly defined by my life experiences as well as my own readings of US history, law, policy, and feminist and queer scholarship of endless varieties (gay studies, second-wave feminism, third-wave feminism, queer theory, social history, educational history, etc.). All came to the fore while I was a doctoral student at Penn State in the early 1990s. I also had the great fortune to work with a very generous colonial historian, semiotician and out gay man, Bill Pencak, who encouraged me to tackle more queer issues at every step of my career: from doctoral student, to candidate, to post-doc, to professor. But at the same time, I was briefly a queer political activist thanks to my involvement with the Lesbian Avengers and the PSU 'Coalition of Lesbian & Gay Graduate Students' (please notice who was left out). Unlike the undergraduate queer group at PSU, the Graduate Coalition was largely a group of gay and lesbian PSU staff professionals and doctoral students with only a few masters students. And most members were fairly docile in their/our political stances. In fact, at one point when we were thinking about addressing the on-going queer bashing that was occurring both on and off campus, one of the highly professional queers advocated doing nothing, noting that, 'We don't want to upset anyone.'

By contrast, the Lesbian Avengers were founded by a sister doctoral student, and we were comprised of fresh/women to doctoral students, all of whom were students at Penn State. We were, quite frankly, sick and tired of the pervasive and occasionally violent homophobia that was daily life at Penn State in the early 1990s. We decided to be much more direct in voicing our complaints. We staged kiss-ins, pamphleted downtown businesses after queer bashings and generally were loud and raucous pests in the name of getting the then university administration to do something to address the pervasively ugly queer hating culture of 'Happy Valley.' 'Upsetting people,' particularly all of the 'nice, white, heterosexual and oh-so-lazy leaders of the university' was precisely our point.

Consequently, during that time and place – Penn State in the early 1990s – there were very few out professors. Bill Pencak liked working with education students and was very vocal about his gratitude to the public school teachers he had as a child growing up in New York City. For those of us who were educators, queer, or both, he provided both an intellectual and emotional refuge – it was safe to do queer work under his supervision. Bill took great joy in all of his work and it was absolutely contagious. He cheered me on, giving me the courage to plunge ahead with 'my queer work' at a time when there was literally *nothing* in the educational policy and administration literatures on queer topics. Bill was a great cheerleader and sounding board – since he had probably read *everything* on most any topic – but because of his readings, he also did not tolerate sloppy work or analysis. For example, g*d help you if you hung commas like a child hung Christmas bulbs on a tree – with great abandon and no discretion – and alas, this was my greatest literary sin.

Yet Bill was not my only influence. I was working toward a Ph.D. in Educational Theory and Policy, with the hopes of securing a position in a College/School of Education. To improve my career options, I worked toward a minor in educational administration, since many of the available policy positions were in teacher education or leadership preparation. Since I lacked the requisite years of experience as a public school teacher, I focused on a research career in the area of public school administration/policy and had the great privilege of working with William Boyd, who was legendary for mentoring generations of young educational policy and administration scholars.

Nevertheless, in a field that has been historically marked by virulent homophobia, I was surely tempting fate, or at least risking failure as understood by queer theorist Judith/Jack Halberstam. As Halberstam notes, *to fail* is to embrace our humanity it is to take risks, including the risk of seeming absurd (2011).

> To live is to fail, to bungle, to disappoint, and ultimately to die; rather than searching for ways around death and disappointment, the queer art of failure involves the acceptance of the finite, the embrace of the absurd, the silly, and the hopelessly goofy. Rather than resisting endings and limits, let us instead revel in and cleave to all of our own inevitable evitable fantastic failures. (Kindle Locations 2460–2463)

In what can only be described as the hubris of young ambition, I wanted to be one of the first educational scholars to conduct research on queer topics in educational policy and politics, as well as educational administration. So much of what I had seen on a day-to-day basis seemed mired in norms of gender and sexuality I thought I could easily spend the rest of my days unpacking it all. Here is one tiny example of how gender and sexuality shaped my own education: My undergraduate teacher education professors *insisted* that the music education candidates dress professionally, which meant women were to wear hose, heels, and either a dress or skirts. This attire presented a never-ending logistical challenge during my student teaching, when I was assigned to teach tuba to elementary students. Given the problems of navigating a tuba and my 'full female regalia,' why were my professors *so* invested in how any young adult looked? Clearly, to begin to unpack this and other questions, I just needed to be in the right, a safer, locale.

Moving on and doing the work

> I argue that success in a heteronormative, capitalist society equates too easily to specific forms of reproductive maturity combined with wealth accumulation. (Halberstam 2011, Kindle Locations 61–62).

While it took me a year to secure an academic post, I was fortunate to 'land' at Rutgers University, located in New Brunswick, NJ. At that time (1996), the state of New Jersey had an expansive anti-discrimination law that covered gay and lesbian people – and it would soon add transgender people to the list of protected categories of people. Given the welcoming political and legal environment, I finally felt safe enough to spend portions of my teaching, research and service agendas on queer issues in education. I had focused much of my early research agenda on conservative political movements in the US and their focus on education policy and politics. I did this, largely because they were virulently anti-queer (as well as anti-black, anti-women, etc., see Diamond, 1995; Herman, 1997). It was a backhanded way to build toward a queer research agenda, but this agenda was one I could not begin while I was a graduate student. The environment at Penn State was too dangerously homophobic.[1] An avowedly queer research agenda would have been far too volatile for a nascent scholar. Once I was settled at an institution and state that, at least on paper supported queer people, I began to move my research agenda toward including queer issues when conducting educational research. I made sure that it was but one of several strands of research all entangled in the very compelling if complicated area of 'the politics of US public school.'

Methodologically, I was trained as a historian, a very traditional historian, meaning I use primary and secondary *written* sources for my data – no interviews (Burke, 1992; Novick, 1988). Since no living human beings are involved, I am forced to look for artifacts or primary sources such as diaries; personal and professional correspondence; newspaper accounts; government documents, including memos, minutes of meetings, arrest reports and criminal complaints, health and safety data, public health records, and court decisions; church, synagogue, and mosque records; as well as unedited sound and video recordings. I also rely on secondary sources, which include scholarly accounts such as biographies; political, social, and/or legal histories; film and audio documentaries; but also autobiographies and memoirs. 'Doing' historical research involves sifting and sorting through these literatures using both primary and secondary sources, shifting back and forth between the two large sets of materials. Historians ultimately weave these disparate sources together to build a coherent *factual* story. Thus, much of my work has been somewhat analogous to a review of the literature – if an inordinately large literature review (see Lugg, 2006a).

I also had and have my own political agenda, which included demonstrating how anti-queer prejudice was part of the woof and weave of public schooling, and, in particular, how devastating this prejudice can be for queer and non-queer children and adults. Such an activist policy agenda is rather atypical for most social science researchers, but less so for scholars in the humanities like history. That said, I had and have a duty to take an activist stance. Whether I liked it or not, my status as an OUT Queer American academic working in a professional field that has been defined by homophobia (Blount, 1998, 2005; Lugg, 2003) means that whatever research I do, it will be seen as inherently political. Consequently, I long ago decided I had best defined the work I did before someone else did it for me (Lugg, 2006a).

A very queer failure

… [F]ailure presents an opportunity rather than a dead end; in true camp fashion, the queer artist works with rather than against failure and inhabits the darkness. Indeed the darkness becomes a crucial part of a queer aesthetic. (Halberstam 2011, Kindle Locations 1356–1357).

For the most part, this queer research stance has served me well, except at the time when I was seeking promotion to Associate Professor with tenure. It is at this point I experienced a profound 'queer failure.' While my tenure package – a box that contained literally everything I had ever written, teaching evaluations, evaluations from outside reviewers, and the low-level internal reviews – had sailed through the internal review process. Once it was sent outside of my immediate school to the larger university, it ran into trouble. The package was strongly supported by multiple levels of review within my school. But at the top levels of the review process, which are outside of the school of education, my package was rejected on the strength of one negative external review (out of a total of 10). While I never had access to these external letters, it was clear from the subsequent grievance process that this solitary letter was hostile toward my queer research agenda, with the letter's author honing in on one single peer-reviewed article. Ironically, this was the only published 'queer article' in a package that contained roughly 10 peer-reviewed research articles and book chapters (most of it solo authored), and 2 single authored scholarly books. On the basis of that one journal article, s/he claimed that ultimately I was writing for 'a small discourse community.' In other words, only other queers would be interested in my work. Since there were supposedly only a few 'dirty queers' running around colleges and schools of education, the letter writer implied I should be a good little educator and exit stage left, leaving the field of research to my non-queer betters.

This failure should have been a fairly straightforward matter to rebut the poisoned penned letter. However, the entire grievance process was delayed by a much larger contractual dispute between the faculty union and the university administration – a fight that took nearly a year to resolve. Before my, or anyone else's, grievance could proceed, this dispute had to be resolved. Nearly a year after I was turned down, I was finally granted a grievance hearing, where I won my case with the help of supportive colleagues and the faculty union. But at Rutgers, a 'win' in a faculty grievance process involving a promotion merely means you must go through the entire promotion and tenure process again. Another academic year unwound with my life in limbo.

This failure, while ultimately not a career ending disaster, did take two years to sort out. I was eventually awarded tenure, but at enormous psychic and financial costs – in permanently delayed raises, permanently delayed monies toward retirement, and permanently ended research projects. At the time, I told colleagues that the experience was akin to shattering my femur or being wide awake for one's own funeral. I would heal, but I would never be the same. And this failure was uniquely, unabashedly, totally, and without any doubt, queer. This queer failure was rooted in professional and personal animus toward my identity and subsequent research agenda. The hostile reviewer exploited the tenure review process – a process that at Rutgers guarantees reviewers complete anonymity – to strike with absolute impunity. At that time and place, it only took 'one bad letter' to sink the aspirations of a given tenure candidate.

Much to my colleagues' astonishment, I had expected to be turned down. Not because of scholarly deficiencies, but because I was a nascent queer scholar approaching an exquisitely vulnerable time in one's career. If I was going to be 'stopped', it would occur at this point. Instead, it was a very brutal 2-year pause. The tenure battle did teach me several things: I had good colleagues at Rutgers and terrific counsel from the faculty union. I also had very supportive colleagues across North America, who all were shocked that the situation was so 'crazy making.'

But in the aftermath of that experience, I completely stopped acting as a polite, nice, white gurl, whose queerness could be conveniently and easily forgotten. With tenure, I had been granted the enormous privilege in having job security – and unless I forced my students to sacrifice goats to Baal on a regular basis, it was and is fairly iron-clad as these things go. I quickly realized that tenure meant little if it was not 'abused' on a regular basis. And so my career proceeded with these understandings.

Moving in queerer and queerer ways: research

Queer theory is oppositional. (Turner, 2000, p. 10)

Since the beginning of that two-year experience (2002–2004) of sorting through my tenure denial and ultimate approval, my work has taken on a distinctly pointed, and more often than not, confrontational tone. This was bolstered by my extensive readings in the law review literature and embrace of a new (to me) theoretical stance: Queer Legal Theory. Queer Legal Theory is an intellectual descendant of Critical Legal Theory, Feminist and Critical Race Theories, as well as Queer Theory. It is a hybrid, drawing on theories from both law and the humanities. While I have discussed QLT in greater detail elsewhere (Johnson & Lugg, 2011; Lugg, 2003; Lugg & Adelman, 2015; Lugg & Murphy, 2014), for purposes of this article, I found it particularly helpful in confronting data, that were shaped by race and sexual orientation, or by class, gender and race, etc., as well as biological sex and gender identity. QLT places queer identity at the center of any analysis, but then assumes that another aspect of identity, like race, may also be shaping the data. QLT has helped me think about the complicated realities of queer experiences and lives while I combed through the historical and law review literatures looking for examples of how anti-queer bias shaped the public school experiences of queer and non-queer students, alike. Additionally, QLT has given me permission, (perhaps license?), to employ more incendiary titles for my publications. By 2003, I was publishing journal articles with the titles 'Sissies, Faggots, Lezzies and Dykes,' 'Thinking about Sodomy,' 'What's a nice dyke like you …?' and so forth (Lugg, 2003, 2006b, 2008).

But by taking a far more overt queer political stance with my research, one that was deeply theoretically grounded, I have run into the occasional ferociously homophobic response. For example, in the fall of 2002, at the annual UCEA convention, I was part of a panel that explored new theories to be applied to the study of the politics of education. After the session, but before the room had cleared, one of the most senior colleagues in the field cornered me and frankly accused me of promoting pedophilia. He could not or would not let go of the delusional slur that queers were, by definition, pedophiles. I probably did not soothe his fury by pointing out that if he cared to look at the FBI statistics, the vast majority of pedophiles were supposedly 'family men.' Eventually, I angrily stomped off, vociferously complaining to any other colleagues who would listen.

This incident was exceptional in its venom, although profoundly insightful as to the condition of academe – at least my little corner of it. A more common experience was having tiny audiences for research presentations or the *cold indifference* by scholars in my field. This was not personal, per se, it was the topic, since sessions devoted to LGBT (lesbian, gay, bisexual, and transgender) issues in education might generate three attendees and five to seven presenters. I also had one job talk during this time of job insecurity, and that audience was completely bi – er, uhm *bi-modal*, if my readings of their body language were correct. Roughly two-thirds of the audience smiled and nodded as I presented a draft of 'Thinking about Sodomy,' which looked at intersection of sodomy laws and teacher and administrator licensure. The remaining third of that audience sat with arms crossed, giving me the frigid 'death glare 2000,' making their displeasure with the material (and me) quite apparent.

But the embrace of Queer Legal Theory had helped me tease out the various ways homophobic and heterosexist bias could and did shape the woof and weave of everyday public school policies. It also was and remains particularly helpful in sorting out my day-to-day realities within academe, not just my home institution, but with my professional associations, which have at times been outrageously timid, at best, and flat out biased at worst (e.g. Lugg, 2010; Tierney, 2010).

As I now slide toward the backside of my research career, I am moving in more methodological directions thanks to the influence of my doctoral students. In particular, I am working with Jason Murphy to develop a more queer methodology for educational researchers to employ – scavenging – or digging through the detritus of queer and non-queer cultures to constructive factual narratives about queer life and US public schools (see Halberstam, 1998; Lugg & Murphy, in press). We are at the initial stages of this project, but it appears to be an elegant way to draw on my training as a historian, former classical musician, and policy scholar as well as Jason's work as sociologist and qualitative researcher. I continue to happily skip through these very queer fields, although it might not be particularly disciplined in the traditional sense of the term for educational administration and policy scholars.

Moving in queerer and queerer ways: teaching

In order to inhabit the bleak territory of failure we sometimes have to write and acknowledge dark histories, histories within which the subject collaborates with rather than always opposes oppressive regimes and dominant ideology. (Halberstam 2011, Kindle Locations 366–367).

Like other researchers, my teaching has been profoundly influenced by my experiences as a researcher – not just in the research data, but in the process of conducting the work, and also in the politics of presenting it at research conferences and, hopefully, getting it published. Most of my classes have been in the areas of educational leadership and politics of education, given the licensure requirements for NJ public school principals. Occasionally, I have taught classes in the area of sexuality and gender, but these are infrequent. I have also taught an occasional historical research class, but this particular class is offered even more infrequently. As a consequence, I have worked to include LGBTQ matters in every class that I teach, as well as issues of race, gender, sex, class, religion, dis/ability, and the like.

Similarly, in the area of dissertation advising, I have encouraged doctoral students to explore issues of diversity, including queer topics, in their dissertations. But, since my students are relatively free to explore the topics of their choice within the areas of educational administration, educational policy, and social and philosophical foundations of education, only a few (out of 30) have embraced avowedly queer work. That said, my tenure battle left its mark – and I am careful to ensure that each dissertation is as rigorous as it can be. While the vast majority of our students (both Ed.D. and Ph.D.) will remain practitioners thanks to family obligations and career paths, a few will become academics.

Additionally, Ed.M. and Ed.D./Ph.D. students will experience career failure, particularly because education, especially public education – from pre-school to graduate school – is savagely disesteemed within the US political culture. Furthermore, some of these career failures will be additionally tied to an individual's race, class, gender/sex, and sexual orientation. While subverting unjust political/social orders via the public educational enterprise is a fine social reconstructionist tradition (see Counts, 1978), sometimes one needs to understand when to make a strategic retreat. For my academic colleagues who are committed to 'leading for social justice,' we fail (again) our students if we refuse to focus on the failures that our students will encounter.

A final point: neoliberalism is busily reshaping the academy as it has most every other American social and economic institution. One on-going failure of my own as well as my research colleagues in education has been to resist the siren calls of the economic mystics. If only we would all conduct research in areas that our elected political leaders are vitally committed to (for the moment), or would better promote a fast-track doctoral program for practitioners, no matter how silly the intellectual results, we might increase political support for our programs and research efforts. It's all highly improbable in an era that is rabidly anti-intellectual and utterly hostile toward public institutions. But the leaders of our public institutions insist that if only we would become more entrepreneurial, our revenue flows would improve. Notice that the language of the market economy has replaced that of intellectual engagement and exploration. And so, we fail again.

Moving in queerer and queerer ways: service

> Failure, of course, goes hand in hand with capitalism. A market economy must have winners and losers, gamblers and risk takers, con men and dupes (Halberstam 2011, Kindle Locations 1228–1229).

Perhaps the most profound change in my professional life came in the area of service. After my own experience with being 'clobbered' at tenure time, I decided to volunteer to read any junior colleague's work who needed feedback on her/his research. And I specifically seek out colleagues who were/are from historically marginalized populations (scholars of color, all women, all queers, religious minority people, etc.). Particularly for those who also embrace social justice work, I want to be sure they would gain critical and timely feedback on their scholarship since it would be their scholarship that would most likely come under attack when they sought promotion and tenure. If their work is going to invite failure, it should not be that they unintentionally ran afoul of the 'norms of academe,' but that they knowingly and joyfully skipped headlong into these walls of oppression, either hoping to break through, or at least creatively subvert them.

Of course, by supporting junior scholars who work at the sociological margins, I am confronted with the realities that some will experience bitter failure. But in a society that glories in white power, endless institutionalized violence, rampant heterosexism, and forms of conspicuous consumption that would make the robber barons blush, this failure is queerly normal. We all need to learn to address the failures that we will experience, not only with the tenure and promotion process, but with the more mundane, everyday failures of having our manuscripts rejected by journals and book publishers, as well as by professional conferences.

That said, failure is a teacher of sorts, as Halberstam repeatedly notes (2011). And by working with colleagues across educational sub-disciplines and generational eras, we can actually 'pool' our individual failures into a larger understanding of how failure plays out in these rarified institutional settings – and work to subvert them. Like public schools and many institutions of higher education, our professional associations can be wildly homophobic at times.

Perhaps the most recent example of a collective queer failure occurred with AERA's publication of *LGBTQ issues in education: Advancing a research agenda* (Wimberley, 2015). Edited by a solitary staff member at AERA, someone who had yet to indulge in any prior queer research, or even conduct the more conservative work in gay and lesbian studies, nearly half of the volume was either authored or co-authored by this editor. This situation of a staffer editing a volume – that is supposed to represent the state of the research field – has not happened with any other AERA sponsored handbook in recent memory. Furthermore, many of the major queer researchers, including almost *all of the major queer researchers of color* in this area, were cut out of the process. The organization's executive leadership deemed the latter group as 'problematic.' The final volume, one that I did contribute to,[2] was much less that it could have been, which was precisely the point. It was designed, somewhat, to fail.

The Queer Studies SIG (special interest group) within AERA had long pressed the organization's leadership to take important political stands regarding the status of queer children in the US. This situation has been particularly acute with the on-going litigation affecting queer adults, which of course, then affects children – both queer and non-queer (see Lugg & Murphy, 2014; Quinn & Meiners, 2009). To this day, AERA remains silent on social justice and queer people. In 2007, the organization's then president inferred that there was no research on queer people and education hence, there was no need to take a political stand (see Baker, 2007; Lugg & Murphy, 2014). I suspect that the 2015 book, supposedly on the best research in the field (cough, cough), was AERA's leadership's effort to get us to 'sit down and shut up' and, hopefully, to 'go away!' That wish is highly unlikely. For those of us who have been deeply involved in these matters – both queers and our non-queer allies – this failure is proof-positive of the hostility that remains at the core of the organization. It is yet another queer failure – in a lifetime of collective failures. Such failure is merely instructive, not destructive, for the *paid pests* infesting AERA membership lists.

Skipping to work or being differently disciplined

> Being taken seriously means missing out on the chance to be frivolous, promiscuous, and irrelevant. The desire to be taken seriously is precisely what compels people to follow the tried and true paths of knowledge production around which I would like to map a few detours. (Halberstam 2011, Kindle Locations 112–114).

And so this meditation of my skipping to Gomorrah has brought me face-to-face with the question most researchers dread: 'So what?' Or as the editors of this special issue more nicely posed: 'Why do you do this work?' Perhaps a better question is why do I willfully, perhaps even recklessly, embrace potential failures?

I start from a quote by my mentor Bill Pencak, who had little truck with the cult of objective history. As he wrote long ago:

> All historians, including those who pretend to be objective, write with an agenda for their own times: to promote or prevent social change, to glorify or vilify particular people or societies. (Pencak, 2002, p. 3).

I will argue that while my life is 'my life,' my work has always been about people and educational institutions and the politics of it all. I am writing to encourage social change, be it merely the little corner of my own social world. I consciously strive to be Dyson's 'paid pestering queer.' Of course, I am also engaged with teaching and professional service also targeted at this goal. But, I am not working in isolation. Instead, I am working (perhaps skipping) with like-minded colleagues through the fields of individual failure in the hopes of radical, collective change. Perhaps our public schools can build a new, and hopefully very queer, social order (Counts, 1978).

Notes

1. One of the worst queer bashings happened during the fall of 1994, when a freshman was attacked while walking to class on-campus (see Marchetti & Reitz, 1995, February 13, for a cryptic reference to the attack). Three to four homophobic white goons had spotted the numerous gay pride buttons on his backpack as they were driving by in an open jeep. They jumped out and promptly kicked his face in. The campus police did nothing, nor did the administration. But the local police arrested the young male attackers, and the county judge threw the proverbial book at the then Penn State students. Only after they were convicted did the administration act, booting the felons out of school. Not because they were violent bigots, but because they were finally convicted felons.
2. I was very conflicted by my own participation throughout this process (see Lugg & Murphy, 2014). Besides the structural hostility to all things queer, the erasure of queers of color is just odious. I ultimately decided to remain involved, hoping that the final product would be so odious that the larger membership would has the same questions that my colleagues and allies have been posing – for many years.

Disclosure statement

No potential conflict of interest was reported by the author.

References

Baker, E. L. (2007). From the president's desk. *Educational Researcher, 36*, 36–37.

Blount, J. M. (1998). *Destined to rule the schools*. Albany, NY: State University of New York Press.

Blount, J. M. (2005). *Fit to teach: Same-sex desire, gender and school work in the twentieth century*. Albany, NY: State University of New York Press.

Bork, R. H. (1996). *Slouching towards Gomorrah: Modern liberalism and American decline*. New York, NY: ReganBooks.

Burke, P. (1992). *History and social theory*. Ithaca, NY: Cornell University Press.

Counts, G. S. (1978). *Dare the schools build a new social order?* Carbondale: Southern Illinois University.

Diamond, S. (1995). *Roads to dominion: Right-wing movements and political power in the United States*. New York, NY: Guilford Press.

Halberstam, J. (1998). *Female masculinity*. Durham, NC: Duke University Press.

Halberstam, J. (2011). *The queer art of failure*. Durham, NC: Duke University Press. Kindle Edition.

Herman, D. (1997). *The anti-gay agenda: Orthodox vision and the Christian Right*. Chicago, IL: University of Chicago Press.

Hutchinson, D. L. (1997). Out yet unseen: A racial critique of gay and lesbian legal theory and political discourse. *Connecticut Law Review, 29*, 561–645.

Johnson, D., & Lugg, C. A. (2011). Queer theories in education. In S. Tozer, B. Gallegos, & A. Henry (Eds.), *Handbook of social foundations in education* (pp. 233–243). New York, NY: Routledge.

Lugg, C. A. (2003). Sissies, faggots, lezzies, and dykes: Gender, sexual orientation, and a new politics of education? *Educational Administration Quarterly, 39*, 95–134.

Lugg, C. A. (2006a). On politics and theory: Using an explicitly activist theory to frame educational research. In V. Anfara & N. Mertz (Eds.), *Theoretical frameworks in qualitative research* (pp. 175–188). Thousand Oaks, CA: Sage.

Lugg, C. A. (2006b). Thinking about sodomy: Public schools, legal panopticons, and queers. *Educational Policy, 20*, 35–58.

Lugg, C. A. (2008). Why's a nice dyke like you embracing this post-modern crap? *Journal of School Leadership, 18*, 164–199.

Lugg, C. A. (2010, September 26). No, we won't *Thinking queerly: Schools, politics and culture*. Retrieved May 15, 2013, from http://cath47.wordpress.com/2010/09/26/no-we-won%E2%80%99t/

Lugg, C. A. & Murphy, J. P. (in-press). Scavenging for data: Queering educational research. *International Journal of Qualitative Studies in Education*.

Lugg, C. A., & Adelman, M. (2015). Sociolegal contexts of LGBTQ issues in education. In G. Wimberley (Ed.), *LGBTQ issues in education: Advancing a research agenda* (pp. 43–74). Washington, DC: American Educational Research Association.

Lugg, C. A., & Murphy, J. P. (2014, August). Thinking whimsically: Queering the study of educational policy-making and politics. *International Journal of Qualitative Studies in Education., 12*, 1183–1204.

Marchetti, M., & Reitz, J. (1995, February 13). Rally targets gay bashing *The Daily Collegian*. Retrieved May 25, 2015, from http://www.collegian.psu.edu/archives/article_db169f49-b756-565f-8a94-f471fba54fed.html

Novick, P. (1988). *That noble dream: The "objectivity" question in the American Historical Association*. New York, NY: Cambridge University Press.

Pencak, W. (2002). *The films of Derek Jarman*. New York, NY: McFarland & Company.

Quinn, T., & Meiners, E. R. (2009). *Flaunt it! Queers organizing for public education and justice*. New York, NY: Peter Lang.

Savage, D. (2002). *Skipping towards Gomorrah: The seven deadline sins and the pursuit of happiness in America*. New York, NY: Dutton.

Tierney, W. (2010, May 13). How do you spell "homophobia"? AERA *21st Century Scholar*. Retrieved May 12, 2013, from http://21stcenturyscholar.org/2010/05/13/how-doyou-spell-%E2%80%9Chomophobia%E2%80%9D-aera/

Turner, W. B. (2000). *A genealogy of queer theory*. Philadelphia, PA: Temple University Press.

Valdes, F. (1995). Queers, sissies, dykes, and tomboys: Deconstructing the conflation of "sex", "gender", and "sexual orientation" in Euro–American law and society. *California Law Review, 83*, 3–377.

Wimberley, G. (Ed.). (2015). *LGBTQ issues in education: Advancing a research agenda*. Washington, DC: AERA.

Finding my critical voice for social justice and passing it on: an essay

Leslie Ann Locke

ABSTRACT

This introspective critical essay elucidates some of the challenges I encountered in my efforts to persist at various levels of education as a first-generation White student from a low-income background and through multiple intersectionalities, primarily class and gender. My lived experiences and transformation from a near high school dropout to a university professor are detailed with particular attention to how these experiences transformed my thinking about my family from deficit to asset, and how I now use this critical consciousness in my teaching and research. Particular attention is paid to the political, social, and educational factors that influenced my philosophy of social justice.

This autoethnograpic critical essay is an incomplete story, and a story in flux, as are all similar constructions (Denzin, 2014; Ellis & Bochner, 2000; Holman Jones, 2005). Within this incomplete story, I elucidate some of the experiences and challenges I faced in my efforts to persist in school as a first-generation White student from a low-income background at multiple stages of education (secondary, post-secondary, and beyond) and through multiple intersectionalities – primarily class and gender. While challenging, my lived experiences propelled me to continue the challenge by carving a space for myself to practice social justice. My story helped me to develop a critical consciousness and voice, which I now use in an effort to assist other educators in their transformation and development of a similar framework. My goal is to interrogate (and at least impact and at most help to reverse) unequal student outcomes. While my story is incomplete, it all started with a myth.

The family myth

Denzin (2014) suggested that autoethnographies begin at the zero-point of origin. This story is no different, as my zero-point of origin is my family. My parents dropped out of high school, got pregnant, and got married all before their 18th birthdays. Although not necessarily in that order, my older sister and older brother had similar experiences; they followed the same pathway. My vantage point, as the youngest child by several years, was informed by family anecdotes of 'should have, would have, and could have.' The most common story of this type concerned education. A frequent lamentation was, 'I should have never quit school.' However, for my family, graduating from high school was forging into unknown territory.

Since no one in my family had a high school degree, job opportunities were limited. My father alternated between driving a truck and shoeing horses, while my mother contributed to the family income by working as a waitress. Both of my siblings followed a similar trajectory. The resultant income was never above a subsistence level; thus, money was always a contentious issue as there was never enough of it. The low wages came in too slowly and went out too quickly, and the financial strain seemed to contribute to the 'should have, would have, could have' storyline. For example, my family members often commented that if they would have stayed in school, they could have different and better jobs, and thus more money and increased options. They seemed to believe in a link between education and fewer troubles. These stories eventually transformed into a myth, where people with high school degrees, and certainly those with college degrees, should, could, and would *definitely* have more – more of everything, including job opportunities. I am not sure if there was a shared vision of what would have resulted if my parents and siblings had finished school, that is, what they would actually be doing if they had diplomas. (Full disclosure here, we are not a close family. I use the conditional tense here because I believe a conversation around these topics may be a contentious one.) But the assumption was clear – my dad would not be sweating the summer away in a big truck that was constantly breaking down, and my mom would not be slinging hash for impatient and entitled diners – according to Liu (2011), they would not be dehumanized and exploited, lodged somewhere near the bottom of the social class hierarchy. However, I don't know if they ever truly envisioned doing anything else. I suppose there was not much time to think about hypotheticals since we were living 'hand-to-mouth' and often 'robbing Peter to pay Paul' as my mother frequently reminded us. Regardless, the underlying moral of the myth – as it was presented to me, and as I understood it – was that finishing school would ensure success, options, and opportunity.

The myth bound me to school, and unlike my parents and siblings, I did not quit. However, what I (as well as my parents and siblings) did not realize was that not quitting and being successful in school were not synonymous. According to the myth, merely passing my classes made me successful. I was confused when I saw some of my classmates studying and working hard in school. I figured, if we were all going to get the same degree, why put in the extra effort? … when it was possible (like me) to put very little effort forth and still pass classes. For me, performance at school was not understood as a means to success; rather, I understood success would be gained simply through completion. This was not much of an issue in elementary and middle school, but in high school things became complicated. While I was passing classes without having to work very hard, I was also often truant, distracted by friends, drugs, and simply having a good time. However, despite these complications, I was passed along, one grade level to the next, seemingly unremarkable yet 'successful.' In fact, despite my frequent truancy, and at the end of my junior year after being told by a school counselor that I had two options, (a) to quit high school because I had too few credits or (b) to repeat 11th grade, I managed (through some creative finagling) to graduate from high school, even a semester early. Without being cognizant of it, through this act, I interrupted a vehicle of oppression; I disrupted the classist business-as-usual approach (Bourdieu, 1974; Ellsworth, 1989) my school was taking – an approach that I later learned pushed my parents and siblings out of the system.

Many of my friends and classmates were planning on going to college after high school. I knew essentially nothing about the processes involved in getting admitted to or going to college, although I knew these decisions would be based on my grades, which were mediocre at best. My lack of understanding regarding college policies is not surprising given there was no college narrative at home, and some of the staff at a high school I attended (i.e. the school counselor mentioned above) clearly did not think I was college material and thus did not waste time talking to me about college. However, as many of my friends were making college plans, I inadvertently heard about community colleges, and that these institutions 'let anyone in.' This open door policy seemed like a good fit for me. I had figured out by this time that if I was going to be anything other than poor like my family, and do anything other than bust my ass, live hand-to-mouth, or rob Peter to pay Paul just to get by, I needed to do 'something.' I did not want to end up like them. I also felt a sense of urgency to do this 'something,' and to do it sooner rather than later or my (class-mandated) fate would be sealed. This 'something' turned out to be college. I was embracing the myth.

I entered a community college one year after high school graduation. Both my parents and I were proud, but confused. Unaware of college course expectations, I enrolled in 21 credit-hours during my first semester. This seemed logical because seven courses was a traditional load in high school, so I thought this could be mirrored in college. Not surprisingly, the highest grade I earned that term was a C. In subsequent semesters, I enrolled in fewer courses, but I was still satisfied with mediocre, and often less than mediocre, grades. The family myth continued to guide my actions, steering me to think if I just managed to secure a degree, it would ensure success. However, if I had at any time decided to drop out of college, claiming it wasn't a good fit, I was uncomfortable, or people at college acted like rich assholes, no further explanation would have been needed for my family. While my parents may have been disappointed, they would have quickly gotten over it and my mom would have arranged a job for me at the restaurant, post-haste.

Like in high school, the family myth was fortified in the community college as I (barely) passed basic requirements and (barely) advanced through coursework. Eventually, I transferred to a local university[1], parroting what my student counterparts were doing, and progressing up the academic ladder once again. At the university, I was influenced and ultimately convinced by science majors that the arts and humanities (even though I found them very interesting) were 'soft' degrees and would not make me marketable. Common to so many first-in-the-family college students, my hopes of obtaining a degree and making money were tightly coupled. In thinking about a 'marketable' major for myself, I tried to imagine what I could do within the 'hard' and therefore 'prestigious' sciences. I was raised in a rural area and had always liked animals, and the local veterinarian seemed to be 'successful,' according to the family myth (that is, he had a big house and a nice car … and my dad often commented that the vet 'had money'). Applying this logic, I decided to major in Science in Agriculture, the pre-vet major, not connecting the facts that I never enjoyed science or performed well in science classes in middle or high school. I told myself that after I graduated, I would apply to vet school. Ultimately, I fumbled through the major, spent a couple of stints on academic probation, but eventually graduated with a Bachelor of Science degree and a GPA of 2.3. The story I had told myself about applying to vet school dissipated somewhere between organic chemistry and calculus. However, despite the fumbling and lost hopes of vet school, I had done it again – I graduated. My parents and I were very proud. I had a degree (a 'prestigious' and 'hard science' degree at that) and therefore I could and should expect success. According to the family myth, the doors of opportunity would soon be wide open for my entrance into the college-educated workforce.

In the field, however, the jobs open to me were in laboratories and in low-level scientific research. To my (and my family's) surprise and disappointment, none of the employment I found paid well. In addition to making very little money, I did not feel confident with this tedious 'scientific' work, and I found it increasingly boring and isolating, and even depressing. It seemed that although I had earned a 'science' degree, I had no real idea of what scientists did. I persisted, however, and eventually landed a full-time job in a lab at the university where I had earned my B.S. While I still did not enjoy the work, this particular job had one significant benefit. As an employee of the university, I was eligible for a scholarship that allowed me to take courses in any discipline, tuition-free. I leaped at this opportunity and enrolled in coursework I found interesting (arts and humanities). Because I was not paying out of my own pocket (i.e. loans) for these 'fluff' or 'soft' classes, as my science friends called them, and since I had already earned a 'hard' and 'prestigious' science degree, I further rationalized my enrollment. Without much conscious effort, however, a transformation was occurring – my GPA climbed upward, and my study habits also improved greatly as I was genuinely interested in the course material. It was not long before I was no longer satisfied with mediocre Cs and Ds.

While the better grades helped me shake off the internal and external judgment regarding these 'soft' liberal arts-focused classes, I was simultaneously becoming increasingly reflective and angry. I thought,

Why in the hell has it taken me this long to figure out what I enjoy learning about? I have a science degree and I hate science – what kind of sense does that make? What good is this degree anyway? Is this my fault? Is it my parents' fault?

'Ahhhh….yes,' I thought, 'it must be my parents' fault. Who else are you supposed to rely on to help guide you?' I became angry with my parents – angry that they would sit by and watch me in tears, frustrated, trying to figure out math problems that they were unable to assist with, angry that they didn't know about college and how I was supposed to get in, angry that they didn't know I was supposed to take these tests called the SAT and the ACT, angry that they didn't know how to support me, angry that it seemed like all they did was show up at graduation, all smiles – having done none of the work, and ultimately, angry that they were poor. 'Lazy asses,' I thought. 'And my siblings, what good were they? They ended up just like mom and dad. Why would they do that to themselves?' For a long time, I could only see my family as deficit, and I blamed them all for my peculiar and bumpy academic journey.

I was pissed, but I kept moving. Fears of an end I was all too familiar with – one that involved me being trapped in a dead-end job and a hateful but necessary relationship, with kids who I did not plan for and could not afford – kept me in motion. Along with boosting my grades and study habits, the post-baccalaureate coursework spurred my involvement in community service, social justice, and education. This involvement seemed to help dissipate my anger and frustration while broadening my perspective. For example, Spanish language courses not only provided me with basic language skills, but also exposed me to many non-profit agencies that worked directly with marginalized and disenfranchised populations, primarily folks from low-income backgrounds and people of color. As a result of the content covered in these courses and the exposure to non-profits, I began to develop an understanding of my own classed and gendered marginalization and disenfranchisement as a low-income White female, and I slowly began to sense the systemic order of exclusion for other groups and how inequality is perpetuated. I also began to feel, grounded in my own personal history, the need to be active – to ask questions and to participate.

Gradually, as my classes and community work continued, the target of my anger, frustration, and interrogation increasingly transferred from my parents and siblings to the schools. For example, the questions I asked myself transitioned to

> Why didn't anyone in my middle school or high school talk to me about college and different majors? Why didn't they figure out what I was good at and assist me in the development of those skills? I could have majored in something I enjoyed! Then I would not be neck-deep in student loan debt for a degree I didn't enjoy and was unable to apply successfully in the field. Why didn't they encourage me to take advanced coursework? Was I tracked? Why didn't they expect more of me? Why did that counselor encourage me to drop out? Where was the college advisement? How do these people, in good conscience, call themselves educators?

Along with my personal inquisition into my own education, in my work with non-profits, I heard about other folks' experiences and desires, their wants for educational attainment alongside their exclusion. It sounded all too familiar. I drew similarities between their stories, those of myself and family, and the myth. Many of the adults I worked with – working-class folks like truck drivers and waitresses – had quit school, yet each wished they had stuck it out until graduation. They had all wanted an education and understood that it would bring opportunity, but something happened along the way that drove them to drop out of the system. Importantly, they *all* wanted their kids to stay in school. I became curious as well as suspicious … it was becoming clear that this wasn't simply a phenomenon particular to my family.

Memories of the accounts my family told highlighting the structural constraints of our education system, such as uncaring teachers who held unempathetic opinions of the poor, and teachers who were too quick to judge minor classroom infractions, started to come back to me. I remembered my parents and siblings who reported boredom, a socially irrelevant curriculum (Gay, 2000; Ladson-Billings, 1995), and feeling frustrated, unremarkable, disenfranchised, and devalued. I remembered when these classist micro-aggressions (Smith & Redington, 2010; Solórzano, Ceja, & Yosso, 2000) came to a head when my mother tried to advocate for better treatment of her son in a high school class, and was ultimately dismissed by the principal. I also remembered the counselor who gave me the ultimatum, quit school or repeat 11th grade, and the stories from my brother who felt repeatedly humiliated by a high school teacher he called [Mr.] 'Chin.' My trajectory into the social sciences helped me to hear the stories of other folks who had similar experiences. It also helped me to better hear my family's stories and understand their educational plight. It seemed like the system silenced and disempowered them, and when they could legally exit school, they did. Somewhere along my path it dawned on me – there were particular norms in schools, and we did not reflect or practice those norms.

As time went on, and as I continued with coursework and working with non-profits, it slowly became apparent that my experience in school was 'marginalization lite.' It was the diet version. Diet in the sense that I made it through, unsuccessful by many standards, but successful by others – I obtained a degree. It also became apparent that many of the folks I was working with, as well as my parents and siblings, may have received the more full-calorie version of marginalization in school, and this is why they exited the system prematurely. I suddenly understood that under schooling was a significant factor that contributed to their shitty lot in life. However, we were not the worst affected. My family actually had many advantages … we were White, my parents were employed, we spoke English, we had mostly reliable and consistent transportation, and we had our full physical and mental capacities, as well as adequate food, clothing, and shelter. It was becoming clear to me that those who do not have these advantages (many people of color and many low-income folks) … had it worse … much worse. The schools expected students and families to have certain advantages and to look and act in certain ways. The racialized, White, middle-class norms (Barajas & Ronnkvist, 2007; Bourdieu, 1974) of the schools became apparent, and I began to see the disconnect between education and justice. But I also saw that for some people, there is no disconnect … there is a direct path, free of holes and detours … and free of marginalization. The generational impact this type of schooling has on families, my family in particular, was coming into view. This was a classist and racist system. Those who do not succeed in the system are not lazy-asses and they are not to blame.

My parents and their messages

As many of the families that I worked with in the non-profits did, my parents also believed in the power of education; they believed that it could, should, and would be transformative. However, because they were not successful in the system themselves, often their sole advice for me in school was 'don't quit.' For some time, I found this directive insulting because it came from people who did not follow it themselves, and who I saw as deficit. 'Do as I say, not as I do' was a difficult edict for me to embrace.

Because we are not a close family, the psychological distance between us as family members made it difficult for me to fully understand the 'don't quit' message. I wanted more from them than a simple two-word summons. I wanted what I saw other kids getting – clear direction – not ambiguity. I wanted help with my math homework; I wanted to talk about the mechanics of English; I wanted them to know about the ACT and the SAT; I wanted them to be in the audience at the talent show. But they never did these things. I now see that they wanted to – but simply were unable. They were working. And they had no experience with this unknown, and unwelcome territory.

My parents did not know the language of 'school,' or have the experience of being successful in the system in order to provide me with the kind of guidance I craved. After considerable time, tears, and frustration, I figured out that it was up to me to decode the only message they could send – the 'don't quit' message. It was up to me to interpret, implement, and sustain this message. And now, partly through their effort, I have the opportunity to honor that message here.

Along with their 'don't quit' message were several other messages my parents sent – many of them were non-verbal. These non-verbals provided mostly by my parents' labor were invisible to me (as well as to the schools I attended). Several seemingly minor events orchestrated by my parents' efforts played major roles in the opportunities I was provided. For example, when my parents divorced, my mother – with intention – moved us to a wealthy school district (the only housing she could afford was a studio apartment – but it was lodged just inside the boundaries of a district where the K-12 schools were continually ranked among the best in the state). When I was in high school, my grandmother bought a new car and she gave me her old one – therefore, I was mobile. My dad often served as my personal mechanic whenever the car needed routine and unexpected maintenance. While I was feeling my way through college, my mom allowed me to live at home, rent-free. And during those years, when she could spare it, she gave me a little bit of cash here and there. My parents supported and nurtured me in ways that they could, but not necessarily in ways that I valued at the time. They also had other assets that are just now coming to light for me.

My mom had, and still has, a profound sense of fairness. Growing up, she would not tolerate unequal treatment – and she was nobody to 'mess with.' I remember at a birthday party I had when I was around 10 years old, a spat erupted among the invitees about whose turn it was during a Monopoly game. One of the invitees started to criticize and marginalize another partygoer, the accused out-of-turn-taker. I weakly participated in the exclusion. Immediately, it seemed (I don't recall my mom keeping that close of an eye on our board gaming), my mom pulled me aside (by the arm) and said, 'Quit that shit. You don't treat people like that. Now go back there and fix things.' The other partygoers were virtually terrified of my mom from then on.

Keeping one's word was also a core value my mother embraced. As kids, my siblings and I knew that if she promised something, she would follow through (although she was careful, thoughtful, and honest about what was within her capabilities to promise). For example, if she said that she would let me borrow her car for the night, or grill hamburgers just how I like them, or give me a few dollars for gas money, she would do it. She never went back on her word, even when integrity placed a burden on her.

Some of my adult friends who have met my mom have referred to her as 'salt of the earth.' I used to think this phrase meant that my mom was just a 'natural' type of person – it seemed to fit, she lived in the country, didn't dress extravagantly, didn't feel the need to bother with much make-up, she spoke directly, and so on. However, after Googling the phrase, I saw the application of this term was a clear compliment and accomplishment. The online version of the Oxford American MiniDictionary (2014) suggested that a salt-of-the-earth person was someone of great worth and reliability. Through her salt-of-the-earth ways, my mom taught me things that may be considered by others to be slightly outside typical gender and class norms. For example, mom taught me that I didn't need to wear make-up; that it was ok to love shoes and the colors pink and purple; to engage in mock WWF wrestling matches with my brother, or challenge the boys in elementary school to 100-yard dashes; that it was ok to wear dresses and go barefoot in the pasture (she did note that going shoeless in the pasture, in particular, was probably a poor choice); and, most significantly, she taught me that I should treat people how I wanted to be treated. While I rarely go barefoot in the pasture nowadays or challenge folks to 100-yard dashes, I still practice many of my mom's salt-of-the-earth teachings.

My dad, on the other hand, was less salty … way less. I don't mean that he was urban, dressy, or concerned about his 'looks,' because he wasn't. But he surely did not fit, and still does not fit, Oxford's definition. I believe that my dad would argue that he was a good father, especially to me. And in some ways, he was good, but not so good in other ways. I was his favorite – he made that very clear – an act my siblings always resented, and rightly so. My brother held this against me for decades, but my sister knew it was a problem, even a character flaw, that belonged to dad, not to me (my sister probably picked up some of that salt-of-the-earthness from mom). I used my dad's favoritism to my advantage when I was young, even though I knew it was wrong. I regret that now. Unlike our mom, our dad treated us differently, and certainly did not ascribe to the same ethics as she did. As long as I whined enough or complained past a particular threshold, I would get what I wanted (in my memory, this method worked 100% of the time). I believe he would argue this giving me what I wanted was illustrative of being a 'good' father. For my sister and brother, if they tried these same tactics, in return they would usually, at a minimum, be denied and sometimes, they would be denied with the addition of verbal or physical insults. My dad's parenting methods significantly aided in the turbulent relationships he had with his kids and spouse. During and after the divorce, my dad used every opportunity to insult and put down my mom (she was fat, she was a cheater, she was the reason for the divorce, and so on). He tried to get me to participate with his bad-mouthing, but I would not do it. I guess some of that salt had finally rubbed off on me. My mom, being the salty person she is, never stooped to his level, she never talked negatively about my dad to me, or likely anyone for that matter.

With these stories, it may seem as though I am trying to belittle or shame my dad; however, none of the above (or below) are family secrets. My siblings and I have had conversations throughout our lives about our parents and the varied parenting we received. While we are not exceptionally close, as we have aged and matured, we have brought our parents into these dialogs. Although it has not always been easy, we continue to work toward openness, understanding, and forgiveness. Even now when we see each other for the occasional holiday, predictably all of us – including my dad (my mom and dad have maintained a friendship of sorts) – get together and talk about what it was like when we were kids. Usually, at least at some points during these reunions, we are able to share good laughs about those times.

As young siblings, we knew and continue to know now that our mom and dad had different strengths and weaknesses in their parenting. My mom was strong in that she knew who she was, and she was a dominant parent. She worked hard to provide for us, set a good example, and be true to her word. My dad, although the weaker parent, also had particular strengths. His love for me (although distorted and disproportionate to his other children) is admirable in its own ways. He also loved animals, and taught all of us how to care for and nurture them.

A particular strength and a credit I give my parents regards work. They worked. My mom worked hard universally (at her job, in the house, taking care of kids and animals, teaching us how to be good people), and my dad worked hard ... sometimes. Unlike mom, who busted her ass in every way, my dad worked really hard at the things he liked and things that were not *too* hard. For example, in the fall, spring, and summer, driving a truck was not as difficult as it was in the winter (Minnesota winters are hard on diesel engines and icy roads are challenging). So, in the fall, spring, and summer, when this work was tolerable and not *too* hard, he worked hard at driving a truck. During the winter, when this work was much more difficult, he did not work hard. Rather, in the winter, he let mom carry the burden of providing for the family financially. Analogous to his children, he liked me, so he worked hard (in his own way) at raising me. He did not work so hard at raising my siblings. Although they passed this on to me inconspicuously; my parents taught me to find the work I like, and work hard at it. Through their labor, effort, and messages, I am able to do the work I choose.

While it took me too long to translate it, I now find strength and resiliency from my family's non-verbal messages, and the 'don't quit' message. It was my responsibility to turn the messages and the opportunities provided by my family into action. Their labor in particular provided me with access to education and opportunity for educational growth. By (finally) recognizing their assets rather than their deficits, I feel that I am helping empower my family – a family that I believe often felt disempowered. Their work and messages empowered me and helped me become more reflective and critical. Feeling and seeing our own inequality and marginalization, and understanding how we as a family were impacted and affected by systemic biases, now informs my work.

Becoming critical

Since 1997, when I began my entry into the social sciences, I have become progressively focused on the issues of bias, exclusion, and prejudice aimed at students of color and students from low-income homes, especially teens and women of color. In the early 2000s, I brought this focus to a master's degree program where I studied the barriers to academic achievement that Latina/o[2] students face in K-12 public schools. Overall, the graduate program allowed me to gain foundational knowledge regarding the systemic and historic roots of educational disparities, not just for Latinas/os, but also for other marginalized groups. I could see more clearly the implicit, institutionalized oppression lingering in our education systems that results in underschooling and exclusion of the poor and people of color.

When I finished my master's program, I had developed enough of a critical lens that I saw educational institutions as functioning from a deficit model (Valencia, 1997) and primarily responsible for the educational disparities between Whites and folks from historically marginalized groups, but I also developed an understanding of how White privilege functions and how I personally benefit from my own set of unearned advantages (i.e. race, native English fluency, citizenship, cisgender, able body). I began to understand White skin as analogous to a credit card – that is, Whites have instant credit or credibility – they do not have to undergo a 'credit check' in our society. Before completing the master's program, but knowing it would soon end, I felt that sense of urgency again, that I needed to do 'something.' The findings and questions raised by my master's research led me to another university to pursue a Ph.D. and continue my social justice education and the development of my critical lens. I chose a university specifically for the department which housed a renowned social justice curriculum and mission. Tenets of social justice were woven throughout the coursework and were embraced by the majority of the faculty. I decided to go into the field of education leadership and policy because I felt that by working with future school leaders and vetting school policy in terms of social justice, I could have the widest influence on improving education for all. That is, working with future school leaders, and helping develop their social justice/critical lens, would ultimately have the greatest impact on the largest number of students. I believed whole schools of children could benefit from leaders with such an outlook.

The university where I obtained my doctorate also had a strong Race and Ethnic Studies Program in the Department of Sociology. I felt a natural draw to the department and I took many courses in this program. Through these sociology classes, I learned about historic, systemic, and institutionalized inequality and its perpetuation, from a different lens. I also developed the ability for deeper critique and reflection. I learned things about myself in those classes that I didn't know. For example, I thought I had a pretty good understanding of racism and how it functioned, then I met Joe Feagin, and all of that changed. It soon became apparent that my understanding of racism and marginalization was somewhat weak and perhaps superficial. Additional coursework and reflection challenged and expanded my nascent understanding. Importantly, Feagin's courses exposed me to the White racial frame (WRF) (Feagin, 2010), a mostly unconscious, but deep and pervasive, way of thinking and acting in our everyday lives that privileges and values Whiteness in all aspects. Once becoming aware of the WRF, it was difficult for me not to see White privilege *everywhere*. It further forced me to challenge my own thinking. Everything I say and do unconsciously and immediately is out of this dominant White frame. (It is easy to get used to White privilege credit.) But the WRF does not introduce itself or knock on your door to let you know it is there. You have to be critical to recognize it. In this coursework, I also learned things about my family, school, community, and government that I didn't know. For example, I learned about the 3/5 clause in the Constitution, the Black Codes, redlining, how Blacks were largely ineligible for the GI Bill, and how 244 years of slavery and 88 years of Jim Crow are the driving forces behind much of the disparities we see today, and many other historic modes and systems that feed present-day inequality and educational disparities.

Not only was my graduate coursework interesting and valuable, but in my doctoral program, I was also given the opportunity to be directly involved with my interests in practice. A graduate assistantship allowed me to work at an Early College High School (ECHS). ECHS programs have been instituted in many states as a social justice and equity-oriented strategy to serve students who historically have been, and continue to be, underserved by the traditional, comprehensive high school model (i.e. students of color, students from low-income backgrounds, first-in-the-family college students, and students considered 'at risk') (Locke & McKenzie, 2015). These rigorous early college programs combine high school and college curricula, providing students the opportunity to earn a high school diploma and up to 60 (and sometimes more) college credits, tuition-free, within four or five years (Jobs for the Future, 2014). The ECHS where I worked principally served Latina/o and African-American students from low-income homes. The majority of these youth, like me, were to be the first in their families to attend college.

My dissertation project was sparked from my work at the ECHS. Latina students from low-income families attending the ECHS were identified by the school administration as the lowest performing for all student groups. In response, my dissertation research was concerned with assessing the ECHS as an appropriate policy intervention for Latinas, a student population ECHSs were designed to serve. This project was a perfect match with my interests and background. Although not the main focus of my study, some of the findings from my dissertation project affirmed much of what I already knew – the parents of the students at the ECHS desperately wanted their kids to graduate and go to college. But, like my parents, they were unable to assist in the traditional ways that could have benefitted their kids educationally and that were aligned with the school norms. But by then I knew better than to blame them or see them as deficit or lazy. And like my parents, these parents believed in education and the education system, even though it may have failed them personally. They wanted the school systems to work for their children; they too saw a link between education and fewer troubles. However, sometimes, the only advice they had for their kids was 'don't quit.'

My graduate programs gave me the vocabulary and a framework to articulate what I had experienced and what I was hearing from my family and others who I worked with. These programs helped me find and form my critical voice, and created a need to help others find and form theirs. My personal experience, understanding of marginalization, understanding of (and anger with) the education system, and varied experience working with disenfranchised groups, has helped fortify my commitment to education for social justice. After graduate school, I entered the professorate because there, I thought, I would have the power to influence and implement, and teach the codes of hegemony, so students could learn to speak for change without compromising their (or my) commitment to it. My plan was to be subversive from inside the 'master's house' (Lorde, 1984); to use the system that exists to change the system because I had come to believe that constructive critique from within can change systemic and historic habits of exclusion. I wanted to focus my scholarship on the K-12 system for two primary reasons. First, I believe most of the responsibility for change lies there, as it is the foundation for future educational attainment. And second, I felt a strong obligation to work to change the K-12 system based on my own and my family's marginalization within that system.

A critical social justice teacher and scholar

As a faculty member, my teaching philosophy mirrors, in part, how I participate in endeavors to increase equity and expand students' critical consciousness. I try to be aware of how to reach students, while being honest to their histories, situations, and contexts – as well as my own. That is, I want to learn from my students, while they learn from me. I want my students to be critical, reflective, and excited by what they learn. I want them to feel safe and comfortable in my classes. But most of all, I want to engage students in reframing their understanding of the conditions they see; to inspire them to become agents of change – authentic educators who are committed to understanding historic and systemic inequities and creating opportunity for *all* students to achieve and succeed. Not an easy transformation for many, and not an easy assignment for me.

Teaching graduate students, many who already teach and lead in K-12 schools, about how and why uneven student outcomes persist and how they are maintained is not for the faint-hearted. Many of my students believe they are already doing everything they can for their students; however, they often locate the sources of underachievement in the usual suspects of poverty, a lack of familial interest in or support for education, cultural inferiority of students and families, or a lack of motivation in students. These are excuses I hear frequently. For example, on the first day of a course on the leadership of diverse school populations,[3] one student described her school's community as ' … a culture of poverty. People just want to be poor. The parents just want to sit around and collect a check.' Most of the other students in the class nodded in agreement with this declaration, exposing their shared deficit perspectives. (At the start of my classes, many of the students have difficulty seeing past the '"logic" of the American meritocracy' [Green, 2003, p. 287]. They tend to cling to proverbial bootstraps.) However, I do not take the easy route of allowing my students to be uncritical and excuse underachievement in the usual suspects. Rather, I challenge their 'truths.' I point to historic, systemic, and institutionalized mechanisms of marginalization and racism. My message is delivered in part by also teaching students about micro-progressions (Stollman, as cited in Glisson, 2014) and counter-behaviors, and to be intentional about change.

As a White scholar who challenges 'truths' and studies issues of racism, injustice, and marginalization, my scholarship is often tested and scrutinized because of who I am – not because of what the findings say, the quality of research, or the quality of analyses. That is, in some academic circles, my Whiteness has a tendency to marginalize my work. I landed my first academic appointment at a university in the Deep South where race, racism, and schooling remain intensely intertwined (Strunk, Locke, & McGee, 2015). This appointment made clear to me that my role in the professorate will not always be comfortable. Although sometimes uncomfortable, I refuse to compromise my philosophy of equity and social justice. I simply cannot disengage from this antiracist work. As Garza (2008) noted, 'Leading for social justice incites … unrest because the hegemonic culture will resist change that provides equity to all …' (p. 163). This culture is resistant because my message challenges the usual excuses, forces them to be critical, and suggests change.

I am White, and I study issues of racism, and I aim to critically trouble inequalities supported by institutional means. As such, I walk a fine line between 'legitimate' findings and not being taken seriously by some scholars, including some colleagues. Some of these colleagues have pushed me to further 'legitimize' my work by collaborating with a person of color (even if that person does not know the content of the study or the related research in the field). While I do frequently collaborate with colleagues of color who know the field and have parallel interests, for purposes of tenure and promotion, I also need to produce scholarship independently. It is primarily with this independent scholarship that I have to explain my positionality and how I became interested in this field, for being White and acknowledging White privilege causes some to question my integrity, my goals, and in particular, my story. While I do not shy away from telling my story, as I sit in meetings and listen to faculty who know little about my work and the scholarship as it relates to racism and marginalization – yet feel compelled to comment on it – I wonder, like Johnson-Black (1995), what it 'would [be] like to cut the shit and say what [I] feel' (p. 25). I struggle with the traditional institutional message of waiting for tenure to find out. My critical colleagues are famous for sending alternate messages such as, 'Don't wait for tenure to be a revolutionary' and 'Your silence won't save you.'

As my story tells, it is not as though I came to my research interests in some novel way, like they fell from the sky or I picked them up at the supermarket. It was through serious critique of my own experience of being on the margins that I discovered some (certainly not all) of the issues experienced by folks from other traditionally marginalized groups were also common to me. It was also through serious and sincere study of racism and inequality. As a White person, it is often assumed that I don't (or can't) know about these things … and given the history of oppressive research, this is a legitimate concern. Some level of discomfort may be (is often) warranted, and expected given this history. I say all of this not to establish or express the notion that I can somehow live outside of the privilege my Whiteness provides, because I cannot (Scheurich, 2002). Our society will not allow it; I cannot 'know' social positions outside of my own; I can study race and racism, and develop much consciousness about them, and I can work to deepen my understanding of them – but these studies, consciousness, and understandings are imperfect and limited; I cannot experience racism like a person of color can. My understanding of marginalization will always be constrained by my many privileges and properties (Harris, 1993), including but not limited to White skin, able body, English-speech, and cisgender (Ellsworth, 1989). However, I may be able to reach a group of White students regarding how they are impacted by racism and privilege easier than a person of color may be able. That is, my White credit may be more readily accepted.

I believe that racism, sexism, and classism are institutionalized in our society. These things are in the air we breathe and the water we swim. These social constructions (Glenn, 2002) are foundational in our society and permeate our lives in all ways, always. However, I have learned, through experience and through study, that I can and should question these constructions. I can and should be critical of thoughts that seep into my brain, unexpected. For example, when I walk my dog alone after dark and I see a young Black male walking toward me, I question why my heart beats faster. 'Am I getting anxious because he's Black? Because it's after dark? Both?' As I breathe deep and work consciously to bring my heart rate down, I summon my self-critique and the WRF. I question the source of this deep-seeded anxiety. It's me, not him. I have been taught to be anxious; this is what we all have been taught. This anxiety, however, reifies what I have learned and unlearned, and that I can, and should, use my privileges to question and disrupt racial and social inequality (Liu, 2011). I can actively critique and resist the negative pervasiveness of our hegemonic culture (Garza, 2008). I believe I have a responsibility and an obligation to be critical. It is also my responsibility and my obligation, as a member of the professorate, to teach others to be critical … to pass it on.

Passing it on

At the time of this writing, I work with students who are teachers and school administrators in a state that is consistently at the bottom of national rankings for education and still supports segregated proms in some high schools. These rankings and customs, along with the reaction of some faculty to my work, confirm that if there were ever a place that needs critical social justice education, it is here. Although never as fast and smoothly as I would like, I believe I am making progress. I am certain I have moved some students, and opened their minds in ways they did not expect, and they are better educators because of it. I have pointed out the injustices that may be active in their own classrooms and schools. This is where my activism mostly manifests itself, in my teaching and through my use of institutional power, from inside the 'master's house' (Lorde, 1984). In my classes, injustices of the past are uncovered, and they often cause people to feel a variety of unexpected and uncomfortable emotions – fear, guilt, and anger are a few examples (Tatum, 1992). While there are emotional risks that accompany critical work (Duncan-Andrade, 2007), we must be willing to confront these emotions and take on these risks as they are the glue that keeps inequity intact. There is nothing we can do to change the past; we have no control over it. Yet, we can, and must, grow from the knowledge. We can and must work for a better present and future. We can and must examine our beliefs and habits. This work is a cognitive and uncomfortable emotional process. Some of the pedagogical practices I incorporate throughout the process include critical reflection and dialog, targeted and diverse readings, and the use of multimedia (blogs, videos, movies, and so on).

Many of my students have realized they may be perpetuating inequity as uncritical, unreflective agents of the institution. And happily, many of my students, I think, are now committed to change. They too are becoming critical. I think I have, and I hope I have, passed on to them a social justice lens. A recent evaluation from a former student included:

> Dr. Locke, Thank you for everything! I have truly enjoyed your class! You have such a sweet, sincere way of sharing the truth, even when we don't really want to hear it, you make us realize we must, it is our duty. Hope I can have another class with you someday! Keep up the good work!

Thus, I think I have encouraged my students to see their privilege(s) and to do something more with it than lead a comfortable, unexamined, and uncritical life; and I hope I have ignited their curiosity and awakened a critical consciousness about creating social change and positively impacting students' and families' lives. I hope they are encouraged to imagine and work for 'a different and more hopeful world' (Green, 2003, p. 297). Like my salty mother who raised my consciousness, I try to pass on to my students 'intense critical consciousness raising' (Ellsworth, 1989, p. 318).

My experience and a critical social justice vision

All the classes I believed to be 'soft' and would not make me marketable ended up being those that shaped and influenced me most. They pushed me and demanded that I become critical. If I had continued in the 'hard' sciences, I would not have been trained to see our social, political, and educational systems in a different light. Moreover, this unintentional trajectory into the social sciences gave me an opportunity to understand that my parents and siblings likely suffered many indignities in schools, including humiliation – they were not welcomed, respected, or heard by this system. I believe these indignities not only impacted their life chances and finances, but also their spirits. Once you are told that you are unworthy, it's a short leap to believing it yourself (Ehrenreich, 2001). As a result, they were unable to realize their full potential (Mantsios, 1995). I believe this aptly characterizes my parents and siblings. However, we are used to thinking of dropouts in deficit terms, as a consequence of laziness, defiance, or deviance. It took me some time to unlearn this thinking. None of these terms aptly describe my parents or siblings, and many others who are 'unsuccessful' in schools. Ironically, these (not so) 'soft' classes begged me to see a vision for my family, myself, and others perhaps outside of what the classist business-as-usual system intended. So much for the 'hard' sciences – I have come to side with Berliner (2002), education is the hardest science of all. Touché!

In spite of their own marginalization, my parents and siblings kept hope in a system that ultimately oppressed and rejected them. Many of the folks I worked with, whether in community organizations or in schools, carried with them a similar hope. Somehow, despite their own negative experiences, they never lost faith that the system could work and that it would bring opportunity for their children. Ironically, for me, these are the people – these myth believers – who influenced my educational attainment, not any particular person inside the K-12 schools. These myth believers were right, educational attainment did provide me with unique opportunities, although given the many bumps and detours on my path, I am convinced that it was accidental rather than purposeful – that is, the schools did little to assist in my success (or my myth-influenced idea of success). Whatever challenges I have faced, I know they are not nearly as challenging as those faced by my parents and siblings, as young people with little education, trying to raise a family and make it from one day to the next. They were right in their 'don't quit' message. And, while it was difficult for me to embrace, if I had not followed their advice, I would not be writing this manuscript. Regardless, the myth carried me through school. But for some folks, that is all 'education equals opportunity' ends up being, a myth. I am now motivated to work for systemic change, not just by my own marginalization, but theirs as well.

While the educational system helped me, it was not in the most direct or intentional way. Oddly, the system that marginalized my parents and siblings (but only treated me with the diet version) has taught me about justice and how to be critical. It should not be this way, indirect and unintentional; rather, it should be purposeful. Educational institutions espouse missions to broaden learning and for the assurance of specific skills. Moreover, schools have been charged with developing the theoretical and technical minds of students for the betterment of society in its entirety. In order to accomplish these ambitious goals, educators must insist that *all* students, regardless of difference, have the greatest opportunity to achieve and succeed in schools. To me, this means schools must welcome students' authentic selves, while providing the freedom for open and critical exchange of dialog and ideas. This is the work that will bust myths, interpret 'don't quit' messages, bring justice through education, and secure a direct link between education and fewer troubles.

We know, and have known for some time, that many policies and practices in schools need to be questioned (Apple, 1993). There is no better time than the present to be motivated by a new political agenda in schools – a civil rights agenda. Teachers and school leaders – as the new civil and human rights workers (Scheurich & Skrla, 2003) – must recognize our society as historically inequitable and that these inequities have been built into our institutions, including schools at every level, public and private. Furthermore, teachers and school leaders must realize students come from diverse backgrounds – very likely different from their own. They must resist the tendency to see some students in their schools as lacking desire, motivation, or ability, and blame low academic achievement and/or educational attainment on the usual suspects of poverty, family disinterest in education, and cultural inferiority, or blame parents when the only advice they can give their kids is 'don't quit.' Rather, they should understand uneven student outcomes as a lack of opportunity to be successful. Striving for equity then is the enactment of social justice, the constant struggle to provide the greatest opportunity possible to all – while remembering that the past affects the present.

Low-income students and students of color in the US continue to be the faces of school failure. Race and class continue to have significant impacts on the opportunity for educational attainment (Lareau, 2000; Mantsios, 1995), and too often are determinants of students' academic destiny (Hoffman & Webb, 2009). We must do better. We owe it to ourselves. Moving from a deficit model that reaffirms the racist and classist norms of schools to an asset model that recognizes the genealogy of students' stories and focuses on the strengths, knowledge, histories, experiences, and identities that are brought to schools (Giroux, as cited by Tristan, 2013) is a good start – although not an easy one. However, without a significant change in the foundational model, it may be that students continue to experience some degree of marginalization – somewhere between the diet version and the full-calorie version.

In our schools, at all levels, we need dialog about 'knowledge' that is socially constructed, debate among multiple perspectives, and inclusion of curriculum that is socially and culturally situated. Lipman (2007) noted, 'these are precisely the kinds of educational experiences students need to help them think critically and ethically about the inequalities that structure their life chances' (p. 47). We all must recognize ongoing injustices and inequities, and we must become acutely aware of the challenges facing students. We must actively work against academic injustices as evidenced by unequal student outcomes. This collective action can make schools positive, empowering, and transformative institutions for all.

Ultimately, as educators, we must strive to authentically understand the zero-point of origin, students, and families; we must be willing to hear and value their stories. Delgado and Stefancic (2001) suggested counter stories 'cast doubt on the validity of accepted premises or myths, especially ones held by the majority' (p. 144). Students and families should not be left to cling to majoritarian hopes and myths about opportunities that can come from schooling. It is time for schools to dispel the myths and replace them with concrete and equitable prospects. In the end, education must ensure success, options, and opportunity and make positive differences in the lives of each student and family they serve. It will require strong leaders and teachers in schools to revolutionize change, particularly change for social justice. It is our responsibility as educators to refuse to replicate inequality in our spheres of influence. Although my story is incomplete and influx and I am unfinished, I am determined to be a contributing factor in this change.

Notes

1. I did not take the ACT or SAT in high school. Because I had accumulated a certain threshold of credit hours at the community college, I was allowed to transfer to the university without ACT or SAT scores.
2. I chose to study the educational issues impacting Latinas/os in particular because, at the time, I was working primarily with these groups in community organizations.
3. Note: The reflections of teaching are those from my first faculty appointment at a university in the Deep South.

Disclosure statement

No potential conflict of interest was reported by the author.

References

Apple, M. (1993). Series editor introduction. In K. Casey (Ed.), *I answer with my life: Life histories of women working for social change* (pp. 1–6). New York, NY: Routledge.

Barajas, H. L., & Ronnkvist, A. (2007). Racialized space: Framing Latino and Latina experience in public schools. *Teachers College Record, 109*, 1517–1538.

Berliner, D. C. (2002). Comment: Educational research: The hardest science of all. *Educational Researcher, 31*, 18–20.

Bourdieu, P. (1974). The school as a conservative force: Scholastic and cultural inequalities. In J. Eggleston (Ed.), *Contemporary research in the sociology of education* (pp. 32–46). London: Methuen & Co.

Delgado, R., & Stefancic, J. (2001). *Critical race theory: An introduction*. New York, NY: NYU Press.

Denzin, N. (2014). *Interpretive autoethnography* (2nd ed.). Los Angeles, CA: Sage.

Duncan-Andrade, J. (2007). Gangstas, wankstas, and ridas: Defining, developing, and supporting effective teachers in urban schools. *International Journal of Qualitative Studies in Education, 20*, 617–638.

Ehrenreich, B. (2001). *Nickel and dimed: On (not) getting by in America*. New York, NY: Metropolitan Books.

Ellis, C., & Bochner, A. P. (2000). Autoethnography, personal narrative, reflexivity: Researcher as subject. In N. K. Denzin & Y. Lincoln (Eds.), *Handbook of qualitative research* (pp. 733–768). Thousand Oaks, CA: Sage.

Ellsworth, E. (1989). Why doesn't this feel empowering? Working through the repressive myths of critical pedagogy. *Harvard Educational Review, 59*, 297–324.

Feagin, J. (2010). *The white racial frame: Centuries of racial framing and counter-framing*. New York, NY: Routledge.

Garza, E. (2008). Autoethnography of a first-time superintendent: Challenges to leadership for social justice. *Journal of Latinos and Education, 7*, 163–176.

Gay, G. (2000). *Culturally responsive teaching: Theory, research, and practice*. New York, NY: Teachers College Press.

Glenn, E. N. (2002). *Unequal freedom: How race and gender shaped American citizenship and labor*. Cambridge, MA: Harvard University Press.

Glisson, S. (2014). Everything old is new again: Storytelling and dialogue as tools for community change in Mississippi. *Oral History Forum d'historie orale, 34*. Retrieved from http://www.oralhistoryforum.ca/index.php/ohf/article/viewFile/552/630

Green, A. E. (2003). Difficult stories: Service-learning, race, class, and whiteness. *College Composition and Communication, 55*, 276–301.

Harris, C. (1993). Whiteness as property. *Harvard Law Review, 106*, 1707–1791.

Hoffman, N., & Webb, M. (2009, June 11). Early-college high school: Modest experiment or national movement? Commentary. *Education Week, 28*. Retrieved from http://www.edweek.org/ew/articles/2009/06/11/35hoffman.html?intc=es

Holman Jones, S. (2005). Autoethnography: Making the personal political. In N. K. Denzin & Y. S. Lincoln (Eds.), *The SAGE handbook of qualitative research* (3rd ed., pp. 763–791). Thousand Oaks, CA: Sage.

Jobs for the Future. (2014). *Reinventing high schools for post-secondary success*. Washington, DC: Jobs for the Future. Retrieved from http://www.jff.org/initiatives/early-college-designs/design-features

Johnson-Black, L. (1995). Stupid rich bastards. In C. L. B. Dews & C. L. Law (Eds.), *This fine place so far from home: Voices of academics from the working class*. (pp. 13–25). Philadelphia, PA: Temple.

Ladson-Billings, G. (1995). But that's just good teaching! The case for culturally-relevant pedagogy. *Theory into Practice, 34*, 159–165. Retrieved from http://www.outdoorfoundation.org/pdf/CulturallyRelevantPedagogy.pdf

Lareau, A. (2000). *Home advantage: Social class and parental intervention in elementary education*. Boulder, CO: Rowman & Littlefield.

Lipman, P. (2007). 'No child left behind' globalization, privatization, and the politics of inequality. In E. W. Ross & R. Gibson (Eds.), *Neoliberalism and education reform* (pp. 35–58). Cresskill, NJ: Hampton Press.

Liu, W. M. (2011). *Social class and classism in the helping professions: Research, theory, and practice*. Los Angeles, CA: Sage.

Locke, L., & McKenzie, K. (2015). 'It's like giving us a car, only without the wheels': A critical policy analysis of an early college programme. *International Journal of Leadership in Education, 19*, 157–181. doi: 10.1080/13603124.2015.1015617

Lorde, A. (1984). *Sister outsider: Essays and speeches*. Berkeley, CA: Crossings Press.

Mantsios, G. (1995). Class in America: Myths and realities. In P. S. Rothenberg (Ed.), *Race, class, and gender in the United States: An integrated study* (3rd ed., pp. 131–143). New York, NY: St. Martin's Press.

Oxford American MiniDictionary. (2014). Salt of the earth. Retrieved from https://books.google.com/books?id=kMRMAgAAQBAJ&pg=PA486&lpg=PA486&dq=salt+of+the+earth+a+person+of+great+worth+and+reliability&source=bl&ots=XhDk_SO8nC&sig=rvw7Yt0QCbl_hu0FbnAFp3ZKaPE&hl=en&sa=X&ei=CGSPVeznN4b_ggSLrpewDQ&ved=0CDsQ6AEwBA#v=onepage&q=salt%20of%20the%20earth%20a%20person%20of%20great%20worth%20and%20reliability&f=false

Scheurich, J. J. (2002). Introduction. In J. J. Scheurich (Ed.), *Anti-racist scholarship: An advocacy* (pp. 1–19). New York, NY: State University of New York Press.

Scheurich, J. J., & Skrla, L. (2003). *Leadership for equity and excellence: Creating high achievement classrooms, schools, and districts*. Thousand Oaks, CA: Corwin.

Smith, L., & Redington, R. M. (2010). Class dismissed: Making the case for the study of classist microaggressions. In D. W. Sue (Ed.), *Microaggressions and marginality: Manifestations, dynamics, and impacts* (pp. 269–286). Hoboken, NJ: Wiley.

Solórzano, D., Ceja, M., & Yosso, T. (2000). Critical race theory, racial microaggressions, and campus racial climate: The experiences of African American college students. *The Journal of Negro Education, 69*, 60–73.

Strunk, K., Locke, L. A., & McGee, M. (2015). Neoliberalism and contemporary reform efforts in Mississippi's education system. In B. Porfilio & M. Abendoth (Eds.), *School against neoliberal rule: Educational fronts for local and global justice: A reader* (pp. 45–60). Charlotte, NC: Information Age.

Tatum, B. D. (1992). Talking about race, learning about racism: The search for white allies and the restoration of hope. *Teachers College Record, 95*, 462–476.

Tristan, H. M. B. (2013, February 6). Henry Giroux: The necessity of critical pedagogy in dark times. Truthout. *Global Education Magazine/Interview*. Retrieved from http://truth-out.org/news/item/14331-a-critical-interview-with-henry-giroux

Valencia, R. (1997). *The evolution of deficit thinking: Educational thought and practice*. New York, NY: Routledge.

An emerging model of family-informed scholar activism

Sophie Maxis, Christopher Janson, Rudy Jamison and Keon Whaley

ABSTRACT
In this article, we, two professors and two students of educational leadership, embrace the pedagogies of community engagement through the ecologies of self, organization, and community. In this article, we explore the development of community-engaged scholars and practitioners through two distinct lenses: faculty who facilitate engaged learning processes and student-practitioners who are enacting these processes in their work. We use an auto-ethnographic technique, our own stories, to describe the will (motivation) and capacity (knowledge) gained through community engagement. More importantly, we provide vivid accounts of marked differences in our teaching, learning, and leadership. As a result, we have become activists in our craft as practitioners and scholars. We also examine how our community-based teaching and learning has been manifested in our current practice.

'If I am in harmony with my family, that is success.' – Ute proverb

Scholarship is intended to inform and improve behaviors, practices, and systems so that our families, organizations, and communities can be healthier and more nurturing. Scholarship is also a primary currency of our work as academicians. However, if our scholarship is informed only through the orienting and culturally loaded frame of the institution of the academy, then only a very small slice of human perspectives and knowledge is put in service of contributing to healthier and more nurturing families, organizations, communities, and the people who live in them. Not only is this myopic lens insufficient, but it is also dangerous as institutions of higher education and their emissaries have often unwittingly done damage to communities due to their propensity and disposition toward assuming an external and elitist 'expert' stance that casts advocacy as something done *for people*, rather than *with them*. As a result of this deficit-laden disposition, even the best-intentioned efforts of scholarship and advocacy serve to undermine capacities for agency, self-determination, and empowerment within individuals, families, organizations, and communities.

The culture of the academy, of higher education, has been rightly deconstructed to reveal its roots in the same cultural soil from which has also sprung conditions of racism, patriarchy, and colonialism. Unsurprisingly then, the history of academic scholarship and research bears these same socio-political stains. It is within this social and historical context that we continue to strive and work toward scholarship that not only subverts this often ignoble tradition of the academy, but also presents a counternarrative through both the products of our scholarship and the process of their creation. What we are seeking is activist scholarship that can allow us to exist and work within and from the academy in ways that are congruent with our value, respect, and love for our neighbors and communities, while also serving to contribute to the 'rehabilitation of the academy,' in the words of our brother Miguel Guajardo (personal communication, 2012).

So we work together to recast and re-imagine scholarship as activist because we seek righteousness. We want to do the right things, for the right reasons, in the right ways. Our scholarship also certainly cannot be separate from our communities. To the contrary, activist scholarship can only occur within the context of community, as we desire for our scholarship to be an instrument of social or political change. For us, that means that our scholarship is not discrete from our service, or from our teaching, *or from our lives and relationships*.

Family stories: narratives as research

Our work together, and the inquiry and reflection processes we apply to our shared work, represents our emerging image of collectively becoming activist scholars. Vital to our developing collective process of becoming activist scholars has been our framing principle/value of family. This frame of family manifests itself as auto-evidentiary, iterative, and dialectic. That is, the more we engage in community development work and activism, the more we recognize how central our frame of family must be. The more we do so, the more effective we are in supporting the development of youth and families and the organizations and communities in which they school, work, and live. Likewise, the more we frame and orient our work through the image of family, the more healthy and whole we become. The more healthy and whole we become, the more humble we are in community.

We are not a team of researchers, or scholars, or activists. We are a family working with other families in community. When we gather together to engage in activism or scholarship, we begin with the understanding that we are joining together in a family reunion of ideas, dreams, and aspirations that we hold collectively about the world in which we live. In contrast to our disparate starting points, commitment to community has led to a convergence of the space we now share with fellow academic activists. In our reunion, family traits that characterize our scholar activism include: our need to connect more authentically in the spaces we share; the desire for meaningful relationship becoming a catalyst for our activism; employing aspects of activism long before discovering the language of activism; our nuanced critiques of education; and activist scholarship as a means to reassert our voices as we shift in and out of spaces of privilege and marginalization within higher education.

We acknowledge the predicament and dualism of activism (D'Souza, 2014), where we have both occupied places of privilege as educators and the tension of marginalization when attempting to dismantle the policies and practices that oppress. Inherent in our work as academic activists is the analyses of systems from which we operate in order to participate authentically within our communities. There is no finality to these analyses; the portrait will never be complete. Thus, our collective work with local and national allies is the operationalization of our convergence as scholar activists and our emerging understanding that conceptions of family should both guide and inform our work and lives in both the academy and our community. The narratives below represent aspects of our individual genealogies as scholar activists. They are individual stories relating our journeys and histories and lineages that have brought us to this work and to each other. These are homecoming stories.

Keon Whaley – the village

My *village*, or 'hood,' was situated within the oft-cited context of drug and violence-laden urban America. At various points in my childhood, I witnessed violence and drug abuse in my home, tragedies among close family members, and experienced temporary displacement of my household. Pop, who I now affectionately refer to as my counselor, crushed my innocent view of the world. Pop had a violent streak triggered by drug addiction and Mom bore the brunt of his struggles. In response, Mom relocated with my brothers and me in tow to a new city to live with extended relatives. She sacrificed to remove us from domestic violence, she experienced even more mistreatment at the hands of relatives, trading in one sorrow for another in order to improve the quality of life for her boys. I did not know it then, but memories of Mom's strength at that time as a lone advocate for us, in the midst of her own suffering, provided the spark for my own activism for and with others. During the midst of my chaotic childhood, I was told that once I made it out, I should 'run and never look back.' The intention behind that directive was my safety, but not looking back would also strip me of the valuable things I learned from my family as well as the wisdom of others in my community.

Despite early family adversities, my parents raised us to be cognizant of our position in America's social and cultural hierarchy. I was not the smartest, the best, the most resilient, or the most focused, but I was told I was by Mom and Pop and I believed them. Mom and Pop used their explicit messages about our social identity and self-worth to encourage my brothers and me while nurturing our abilities to advocate for ourselves and with others. Moreover, our parents welcomed the community's involvement in our upbringing. They encouraged community members and educators to teach us things they could not and to reinforce their efforts to raise our consciousness. Collectively, those in my village were generous in their efforts to teach me about people from the past who challenged the status quo in the fight for social justice. Mom also taught me that being a Black man in America warranted a higher level of personal and professional astuteness unless 'you want to be digging ditches like your Daddy, Son.' This was the motivation behind their strategic over-praise. Consequently, I always felt that I had to do *something*. I had to do more. And I believed that I could.

Our household was not perfect, but we were never allowed to use our imperfections as an excuse for failure. Instead of allowing the family challenges to be a hindrance to our progress, trials became our launching pad as we persevered and overcame challenge after challenge within our family and community. This practice in overcoming, in perseverance, was preparing me for the unseen barriers that exist for Black men in the U.S. 'Opportunities [and resources] are few for someone like you, Son, because you been taught to walk with your head up high.' Whenever I articulated to Pop that I wanted to be like him, he countered with 'you will be better than me.' Mom constantly assured me that my intelligence and potential were not enough to persevere through my three strikes – being Black, male, and in America. With words like, 'you're too smart to be doing such dumb [stuff]' or 'think boy – common sense ain't common, huh?,' she was preparing me for the reality that, as a Black man, my margin for error was slim.

My acculturation as a Black man was decorated with vivid storytelling from community elders who, affectionately called *OGs*, graciously offered wisdom and life lessons to willing observers. I was often the only youth present among the congregating OGs. Crafty innuendoes hurled at my potential sexual activity, whether active of not, made me a little uneasy. I idolized the OGs as they often shared their perspective life stories and lessons about the possible obstacles for a young man losing sight of his dreams in order to bask in teenage glory. We called it *spitting game*. As story after story and warning after warning were told, I began to feel comfortable just listening. It was not my time to talk. It was my time to soak 'game.' In essence, it was my time to be the student and learn how to navigate the land mines of being a Black man in America from among the most respected and knowing sources of wisdom within the village – the elders.

On one evening, a particular OG kept my attention, not by what he said, but by what he did. With a cane he crafted from an old tree branch in his yard, he made the most perfect hole in the ground. Prompting a brief pause from the group conversations and laughter, with unforgettable *gravitas* and rarely expressed angst, he summoned for my attention, 'Youngblood!'

You are never called by your given name until you earn it.

'You see this hole?'

'Yes', I replied.

'You see this stick?'

'Yes.'

'No matter how hard I jab this hole with this stick, the stick'll break before this hole will. That hole will only get deeper and wider.'

I snickered, but his countenance never changed.

'You went too deep for him, Clyde!', I heard an OG say.

I shook my head and wondered if he was talking about sex. Was he telling me how to please a woman? If not, who or what is the stick? Who or what is the hole? That illustration has resonated with me during every developmental phase of my life. I am the stick. The world is the hole. The angst that the OGs allowed me to witness mirrored the pain and anger I felt as a young man. They tried to make their marks by jabbing at the hole. Mr Clyde never told me to stay away from the hole. He told me to find another way to shape that hole so that the hole does not break me.

I learned still more lessons about what it means to be a Black man from the hood vicariously from childhood friends. In many ways, the village, inhabited by rich wisdom and admonitions from family and community sages, saved my life, yet did not seem to do the same for my peers that I left behind. As a Black male and because of the village, I worked hard to succeed academically. I would not be broken despite the inequities within the public school system and society at large. My resilience, though, was in contrast to my childhood counterparts, who came from similar circumstances, but experienced less success in society. Thus, the portrait of my activism emerges in part from the background of childhood friends who were not less capable, but less fortunate in how they experienced life in and beyond the village as Black males in America.

I often dream of what might have been for my childhood friends if they, like me, left the village more unbroken. These dreams of possibilities unrealized and potentials untapped compel me to act for change and also prevent me from engaging in scholarship detached from the memories of my childhood friends and the forces that moved to break them. I remember friends with brilliant intellects who lacked academic motivation and had very few teachers who neither recognized their potential nor were able to pull it out of them. I remember friends who only heard about how 'bad' they were. One of these 'bad' friends once asked me what type of kid I thought he was and I replied simply that he was like any other kid. While fighting back the tears welling up in his eyes, he replied 'You are the first person that didn't tell me I was bad as hell.' A stout, imposing young man he was sitting in the passenger seat of my car, all but saying that his life was a self-fulfilling prophesy. Just one year later, he began serving a sixteen-year sentence in a privately owned federal prison.

It is these reflections on my childhood that have informed my conception of being an activist scholar. This conception is rooted in growing more comfortable with the uncertainty of evolving meanings and shifting perspectives. I am left with more questions than answers for what set me apart from the tragic, yet common outcomes of many of my peers growing up. In contrast to these stories of my childhood friends, my story is sadly remarkable. How did I not break? Was it because I listened more closely? Was it because I learned that my elder's stories had a purpose beyond entertainment – that the stories were really an instruction manual for survival as a Black man? Was it because Mom and Pop humbly and wisely allowed others to impart wisdom and guidance? Why was I the only youth who spent time with the elder OGs? I first asked these questions through a lens of guilt, but now I ask them in the spirit of critical self-analysis that informs my current journey into the academy as an emerging Black male scholar who sees a purpose, an activism, to my scholarship.

My development as a learner in public education, and my subsequent education career, paralleled the socialization many other Black males experience in education and society overall. It was as an educator that I experienced the disenfranchisement many of my friends had growing up. I erroneously assumed that I would be a cultural commodity among the mostly White, middle-class, female teachers in public education. Surely, someone who looked like me could save young Black men just by being a welcome sight among the underrepresented. Not so fast. I learned within my first month as a novice teacher that while some youth were encouraged, many others like my childhood friends were practically neglected academically and socially. I spoke out. My desire to support the underserved was viewed derisively by my colleagues and school leadership.

I saw a need to more effectively support young Black men, but I was not emboldened to seek educational justice on their behalf at the time, nor did I have the right skills and support to do so. I felt boxed in and helpless. I would not endorse the culture I perceived in my school as rationalized, leaving some children behind through the pervasive assumption that some children *wanted* to be left behind. I resigned.

I believed that my departure from public school teaching was about being noble and not contributing to the 'school to prison pipeline.' In hindsight, students in that school – just like my childhood friends – needed me to speak up loudly, to pull a community together to fight for education as a social justice issue, and to place our school system on notice that all students matter. However, I was neither ready, nor able to lead that type of activism. Now, I am farther along.

My journey as a scholar activist has been both a blessing and a curse. The deeper I delve into the analysis of policies, practices, and status of student outcomes, the more blaring the injustices of education seem to be. When I was a teacher, I was unable to articulate my growing frustration with the dismissive treatment of poor youth by the education system. There were other teachers and some administrators who also expressed discontent toward the neglectful educational system. However, their discontent rarely moved to action. Were they experiencing the same paralysis as I was? Or did they simply care more about their jobs than the welfare of students? Regretfully, I began to sing the same song of student, family, and community deficits. That Black youth are only a product of their dysfunctional environments and collective apathy contributes largely to that dysfunction. My contempt and discontent toward the educational system, and my hopelessness toward changing it, grew increasingly unbearable.

In the midst of my hopelessness, things changed for me. I was able to find others who had also been disgruntled, but were now *doing* something. When I met Drs. Janson and Maxis, I observed that they had moved beyond their outrage and critiques of the injustices in our schools and communities. Instead of being paralyzed by frustration and hopelessness, they were bringing people together who were closest to school and community injustices and inequities and providing pedagogical opportunities and processes for them to learn and grow together so that they could collectively challenge their organizations and institutions to better meet their needs and serve their ends. With others including other graduate students and community members of all ages, they were serving as resource brokers. And those resources were the hopes and dreams of the community. It is when I joined them in this work, that I first experienced scholar activism. Now, as I have grown through the work myself, my activist family has helped me reframe my history with education in order to find new purpose for my struggles professionally.

I imagine the blacksmith's hammer pounding on a piece of steel, shaping it into a useful precise instrument. Visualize both instruments simultaneously sharpening one another, yet alternating roles (the hammer or the piece of steel). The most sharpened one is the one most in need. On some days, I am the sharpened one. As a scholar activist, I represent my childhood friends who were overlooked as valueless by a society that just saw them for what they did not have. I hold close to me the reality that I was not far behind them on the pipeline to prison. I may have 'made it,' but I was not the most intelligent or the most resilient among us. Unlike many of them, though, I had the collective support of a united village.

Now I act on behalf of those young Black men who were constrained and blocked from becoming the men they deserved to become. My activism is within the academy, leans on what sustained me in my neighborhood as a child: my extended family both biological and spiritual. I have assembled a family around me now in the academy. This family, including my co-authors, has helped me understand that my own childhood challenges are my strengths. I had to grow up in an impoverished neighborhood. I had to struggle within the system of public education in order to witness the physical and symbolic assault of Black youth in urban America. It is my own rehabilitation of my own story and its convergence with my love for those with whom I advocate that sustains the fight for me now. I need to love and my scholar activism must come from a place of love and hope, rather than anger and despair.

Rudy Jamison – searching for home in relationships

Academic activism signifies my return to *home*, where values, specifically, a fundamental need for relational authenticity, have always compelled me to pursue congruence among my home culture, career development, and academic development. Relational authenticity is not easy for Black men in America, even among ourselves. We have been bombarded with, and subjected to, narratives that seek to set us up as competitors with each other, rather than brothers in relationship. However, my lived experience is much deeper and much more life-affirming than the shallow veneer of the 'crabs in a bucket' metaphor for the Black community. Instead, mine was a childhood of crab boils in the backyards and homes throughout my neighborhood and the friends and families that always welcomed me with hospitality and supported my growth.

My early work experiences in the corporate world were fraught with metaphysical angst and remorse as the values and virtues most dear to me oftentimes contradicted those that were deemed necessary for career success. As a Black man in America, I had to balance the pressure to acquiesce to the indignities and systemic inequities, suppressing my more collectivist home culture in order to succeed individually in a 'Eurocentric' professional landscape. As I've transitioned to becoming an academic, this dualism also holds true for me and many of my Black peers, who care deeply about what happens to and in our Black communities, and so are pursuing careers in an academy that does not acknowledge the Black experience as one of significance. Consequently, although the focus of my scholarly inquiry is a strategic and appreciative inquiry into the lives and experiences of Black men, my scholarly activism emerges from the relational authenticity, social hospitality, and invitedness of *family* I have learned to co-construct and model with Sophie, Keon, and Chris while we commit to and engage in the development of ourselves, our organizations, and our communities.

My commitment to integrate relational ethos into my academic activism is fueled by personal experiences with and observations of the unearned privileges of individualistic, Eurocentric male dominance in contrast to the more collectivist orientations of marginalized populations in the work place. Growing up in a relatively low-income neighborhood, my upbringing was shaped by a set of well-defined cultural values, where honesty, authenticity, loyalty, and altruism comprised our shared sense of community. In my neighborhood, to lie, deceive, or even withhold information was akin to blasphemy. From my observations within the world of work that I would eventually enter, the cultural values that I was familiar with were often elusive in the relationships that developed.

Much of what perceived Eurocentric professional behavior exemplifies is counterintuitive to the life experiences of many in underprivileged communities. Coming from such communities, I have had to navigate relationships within the world of work, sometimes learning the hard way about assimilation, yet always mindful of the environmental nuances within professional culture. In the following passages, I reflect on defining professional experiences that were extremely discouraging and disappointing because of fragmented relationships and foreign cultural customs. As disheartening as these experiences were for me, they were the catalyst to the path of academic activism that I practice currently. Although previous work roles have been challenging in this sense, I have learned to position myself in spaces that complement my values, spirit, talent, and aspirations.

Upon graduating from an HBCU with a Bachelor of Science degree in Biology, I returned home to in Jacksonville, FL, desiring to teach at a predominantly Black school. Once there, I was disturbed to learn that due to mandates forcing schools' teaching staffs to reflect our city's racial demographics, I was forced to accept a position at a predominantly White school, but it at least came with a coaching opportunity. However, as much as I tried, authentic and genuine relationships seldom developed for me throughout the department or the school. Very little about the school's climate felt like *home*.

Looking back now, the academic activist in me was developing during this stage of my teaching career. I worked hard to create a sense of family and camaraderie within my classroom and coaching environments and for the first time those efforts were more than intuitive. They became more and more intentional. My talent for teaching had come easy, but now I was allowing for learning in ways that involved more youth voice and it resonated with my students and athletes.

A few years into my teaching career at the predominantly White high school, tensions with supervisors grew because of divergent perspectives around 'doing things right' and 'doing the right things.' The school's academic culture adapted to rigid rules without regard for what was best for students. The athletic program evolved more deeply into dominant Eurocentric cultural approaches, where the style of play, on- and off-the-court behavior, and dress all reflected that of White players and coaches to the exclusion of others who were not part of the dominant culture.

There was a sense that leaders were more concerned about maintaining the 'system' rather than the students the 'system' served. I experienced significant disconnect with key leaders who tended to be procedure driven, with low expectations of players, superficial relationships with parents, and passive-aggressive communication styles. There seemed to be no willingness or capacity to draw upon my skills and talents in order to support the broader program goals and best interest of students. I knew that I had so much to offer the school and it was frustrating not knowing how to contribute in a productive way. My pushback to the standard operating procedures proved to be in vain. I was eventually fired from the coaching position and given an explanation of 'the program would like to move in a different direction.' In hindsight, I could have done a better job of managing this relationship. At the time, I did not have the consciousness or the aptitude to see other possibilities or paths. Regardless, when I think about it now, it was extremely clear that this was not *home* for me and it certainly did not feel like *family*.

At the end of a 10-year career in K-12 education as a teacher, coach, and administrator, I pursued work in corporate America. I felt that if I could master the art of sales, this would afford me job security. A prominent pharmaceutical sales company eventually hired me. It felt like Christmas: an attractive compensation package including quarterly bonuses, a company car, an expense account, and daily deliveries of gifts and marketing material for doctors' offices. This was a far cry from my public education career. At the same time, I remember being on the company's massive campus thinking everyone looked like 'Barbie and Ken' – young, thin, attractive, and White. However, I refused to use differences as an excuse for failure and immediately immersed myself in product knowledge and company culture. I did very well throughout training and was selected 'Most Valuable Salesperson' by my peers in the training class. However, the hyper-competitiveness did not feel like home. This was 'crabs in the bucket.'

Despite the demonstrable success I had in this sales position, I again began feeling incongruent with my work culture and environment. I simply did not privilege the work culture and leadership of the business world that concerned itself most with profitability over principle. I often felt that we could have done much better if we had taken a pro-people approach, and focused on patient profiles, physicians' concerns, and script-writing habits. Although there were some sales professionals that were truly interested in doing what was best for the client, most focused on money and mobility.

Anything that resembled the values of my home or community was scarce and unappreciated. Almost all attention was dedicated to processes and little addressed human development. Whenever I asked about or suggested ways to humanize the work, I was figuratively told to 'mind my business.' I remember discussing with my manager about my career path and developmental ideas. She trivialized my ideas, while concocting time-consuming tasks, busy work that was coded as 'stretch assignments,' to keep me out of the way. As I reflect on this and subsequent corporate experiences, they failed to fulfill my need for meaningful development, authentic leadership, and rich relationship. I grew tired of the lack of professional development and cultural climate. I eventually left this system for entrepreneurial endeavors. If I could not find a work environment that I could call *home, with people who felt and acted like family*, maybe I could build it myself.

Hustling as an entrepreneur continued the demanding processes that I encountered as a Black male where internal conflicts pitted my conscience with Eurocentric business culture. I noticed more emphasis on socially constructed aspects of professionalism related to areas such as behavior, dress, language, and traditions, but a desperate lack of familiar cultural values in the work environment. I saw that American professionalism did not value what was right, but what was 'White.' With each job and entrepreneurial effort, I felt rejected by professional America, unfit to climb the hierarchical ranks that elude so many Black men like myself. However, as I reflect on my narrative, I realize that in an unconscious, visceral way, I rejected the 'system.' Ironically, the values and beliefs that were a part of my early family and neighborhood life took precedence over my desire for position, power, and money. It is in my resistance to rigid corporate culture *as a Black male* that I matured personally and professionally.

Finding congruence with work may never happen for some and, if lucky, be short-lived for others. Thus, as a Black male, I find academic activism must include reciprocal relationships that allow for all in them to grow. I develop my own relational skills while supporting others to do the same – just like a healthy family. It is only together with others, with Sophie, and Keon and Chris, that our academic activism can more fully emerge and support our collective efforts to help create the conditions for marginalized populations to educate, equip, and empower themselves. I still hold on to some business roots and seek to activate our relationships in order to help Black men and women develop the cultural knowledge and tools necessary to problem solve and navigate the cultural land mines of career development in Eurocentric environments. Within the context of the academy, our work through our relationships has provided space for Black males, and others who have been oppressed, to imagine a different way of being, acting, leading, and using power. Our goal is not to simply supplant overrepresented White leaders and academics; what we want to do as academic activists is to supplant the procedures, policies, and structures of the academy that serve to maintain and reproduce systems of inequality in the first place.

I feel more congruence now in our work together. I am now a doctoral candidate in an environment where my aptitude is better understood and appreciated, advancement opportunities are available, and relationships are authentic and mutual. Maybe it is that I am in my sweet spot, and in being there, I am better at developing and sustaining authentic relationships. I am in a space that has certainly changed my personal and professional trajectory. The pivotal point here is that space (home), people (activists), and organizational culture (values) matter. This ideology of space, people, and organizational culture cannot be limited to idiosyncratic advancement but must be shared with the least of these in an effort to build civic and social responsibility within community. Sophie, Keon, Chris, and I are developing a new way of the academy through our relationships. We are practicing democracy and in doing so, we are having the bold and necessary conversations about how race and gender influence our relationships, expectations of ourselves and others, and the ways we lead and learn. Our relationships consist of respect, trust, authenticity, commitment, responsibility, and philosophical alignment. There is a mutuality that exceeds reciprocity and amplifies a more constructivist collaboration. We work at supporting one another; we are receptive to criticism, and deliberately look for ways to make each other better. There is an egalitarian spirit and a learning posture that encourages openness, values vulnerability, and magnifies teachable/learnable moments.

Academic activism is my home, which welcomes my voice, challenges my perspectives, fosters fellowship, and inspires me to be better for my community and me. I am a member of a family of academic activists who purposefully create a set of conditions that feel like home. When we convene, work, and play, there is a genuine comfort to foster trust and confidence and put forth our authentic selves as scholars, learners, and leaders within the academy and our local community. I am a firm believer that everyone wants to be accepted, learn, contribute, and be recognized. Once these conditions for growth are met, by extension, we can become productive academics and activists.

Sophie Maxis – the sources of my activism

My family's migration to South Florida during a second wave of movement into the US from Haiti's dictatorship during the 1970s influenced my early appreciation for community activism. The fear of many Haitian immigrants during this time was the news of loved ones who, while awaiting reunification in America, may have been injured or killed during political unrest and violent demonstrations. As the first of my parents' children to be born in the US, I represented their hope as they sought to reunite our immediate family still living under the oppressive Haitian regime while struggling to establish roots in the 'pays étranger,' foreign land. The constant worry for the safety of our loved ones in Haiti would not be assuaged for more than 25 years, when my two remaining siblings migrated to the United States. Hope in the midst of such struggle was necessary as my family, like many of our neighbors, attempted to recreate a sense of community that was the way of life in their beloved country. The sense of community and collective consciousness often seemed elusive in this individualistic host country. The urgency to maintain a sense of community framed my conceptualization of collective responsiveness. Thus, the socio-political influences of being raised in South Florida contributed to my early understanding about collectivist consciousness and advocacy.

In contrast to the civil rights gains in America, Haitian American activism was being fueled by heightened political unrest in Haiti and the discriminatory changes in US policy toward Haitian nationals seeking asylum. I recalled the climate of both cultural exploration and cultural clashes in South Florida, as the negative regional attitudes toward Haitian grew with their influx into Miami. The schooling experiences of many Haitian children enrolled in South Florida schools during this season were sometimes wrought with social isolation and violence. As a result of the cultural differences and negative attitudes toward students bearing cultural markers of being 'other' than fully American or non-English speaking, my siblings adapted a disposition of self-advocacy and advocacy on behalf of the 'others' at our schools. Among my four siblings that attended public schools in Miami, we were careful to protect each other and look out for others who may have been teased and bullied for standing out socially. Being a child of that era and witnessing the Haitian community's strength of spirit during adversity shaped my disposition toward community activism and advocacy.

Notwithstanding the negative perceptions toward Haitians during the 1980s, my formative years in South Florida schools offered a culturally and linguistically rich experience, which often extended beyond the building level. Although I entered formal schooling when the celebratory mood from the recent national Civil Rights victory still lingered, Haiti was in the midst of political upheaval while South Florida was being transformed by the regional bilingual education efforts. I remember vividly the explicit messages of liberation that were passed along through songs, neighbors, and advocates who seemed much more engaged, both in and out of the school context.

I attended community schools, whose names were developed or changed to memorialize African-American heroes such as Martin Luther King Jr, Phyllis Wheatley, James H. Dillard, and Booker T. Washington. On the heels of the Civil Rights victory, teachers were more explicit about the need to remain politically and civically involved, lest we lose ground on our recently gained rights. Subsequently, my primary education was set with experiences such as reciting poems by Black authors, learning about our 'unalienable Rights,' singing Freedom songs after the Pledge of Allegiance, and bilingual instruction in school and at home. I received an early education of models for social justice, advocacy, and activism through the very institution, public schools, that now seem more cautious about endorsing the ways in which education and activism intersect. My formative years provided good soil for my current engagement as a scholar activists in higher education.

A natural progression for my activism was a career in education at the PK-12 and post-secondary levels. Much of my education career has been situated in diverse school communities. The inequities in public schools that I observed during my early teaching career and the intellectual benefits I derived from my history of community-centric schooling contributed to my tendency to ask more of my students than the mastery of content-area knowledge. In my previous role as a teacher in the traditional PK-12 setting, my desire was to privilege relationship building to the degree that the students with whom I engaged were able to access their own agency to think and act freely toward the greater social good.

My education career has led to my present-day activism in a large, urban hub, with fellow scholar activists in higher education. As I reflect on my work as an activist scholar, the act of reflecting keeps me from becoming too far removed from the sources of my work and activism. I understand more fully what shapes me and drives my passion to labor for more equitable systems and stronger communities: a deep sense of family, faith, and self-discovery resulting from my engagement of reflective practices and activism.

This same reflective process continues to guide my teaching and leadership practices. Activist academic colleagues describe this work as becoming a way of life (Guajardo, Guajardo, & del Carmen Casaperalta, 2008). I suggest that my way of life became the work, which may explain the natural fit between my teaching, learning, and leading in higher education and my disposition as an activist scholar and community activist.

As an educator and emerging leader in higher education, my scope has broadened to model and encourage relationship building to the degree that my graduate students will become socially conscious professionals who embed themselves within communities in ways that increase community self-agency and collective problem-solving. An overarching prompt in my preparation of educators, who will most likely serve in diverse school communities, is the constant gauging of self to assess the extent that their knowledge and expertise are able to help others access their voice and act on their (students, families, and communities) volition to problem solve. To maintain a neutral stance as an academic is a false assumption that we are not a part of the system that we seek to examine in our scholarship (Siplon, 2014). Thus, the model of community of engagement that I engage in supports the ways of knowing that result from participating (Rodino-Colocino, 2012), is characterized by a commitment to help others reclaim their voice, builds upon student capacity as learners, and reminds a pre-service educator of his or her power to think and act freely toward a more just and equitable society.

My desire to make a difference beyond the academy through constant analysis of whether policies, practices, and theories empower or disenfranchise (D'Souza, 2014) undergirds my commitment to critically analyze and then act (Rodino-Colocino, 2012). Moreover, activist scholarship symbolizes my reclamation to think and act freely in contexts where my learning, voice, and entitlements have been devalued historically as a person of color and social justice advocate.

Chris Janson – spirit, vocation, and family

When I think about what being an 'activist scholar' can mean, I think about what lies at the source of my own work and life. The theologian Frederich Buechner explored a meaning for *vocation* that transcends the simple term for one's trade or occupation or even feelings regarding the suitability a person feels they have for a particularly occupational path or career. Instead, Buechner described vocation as being the 'the place where our deep gladness meets the world's deep need' (Buechner, 1973). In doing so, Buechner moved the reality and idea of vocation from the material to the spiritual. Vocation, then, is not just the condition of having paid work, but is a call in a spiritual and ontological sense. Buechner further contextualized this spiritual summoning, writing that 'The kind of work God usually calls you to is the kind of work (a) that you need most to do and (b) that the world most needs to have done' (p. 36).

At the source of my own work within and from the academy, what motivates me as a scholar and as a professor has converged over time with the same things that motivate me as a neighbor, as a friend, as a father, and as a husband. I am moved by relationships through which I can change and grow. In turn, I strive to build and sustain relationships so others might change and grow too. The importance of relationships to development and to the learning and leadership required to support that development is a deep source of my own activist scholarship. From this source, I have moved closer and closer to what I now understand as my own vocational point of intersection: my evolving understanding of and appreciation for the wisdom and gifts that exist in communities (McKnight & Block, 2012) and my commitment to working with others in order to help them develop their own approaches to liberate their wisdom and gifts in order to meet their own needs and become more healthy, more joyful, and more purposeful.

My call toward vocational intersection has been strengthened and magnified by the idea that collective efforts to support the health and development of individuals, families, organizations, and communities are more helpful and effective when conceptions and values of the family are central to them. As I shifted from work as a public school teacher and later school counselor to work in the academy as a professor, I maintained a commitment to working closely *within* communities. Looking back now, I recognize that my paradigm was limited and limiting. I was working from examples of community-based engagement modeled by other professors. Their examples were generally based around the importance of maintaining close proximity to practice or motivated by a sense that university students and the university itself should contribute in some way to the communities that surround them. Theirs, and mine, was essentially a service-learning model sometimes cloaked in the expressed belief that we were *advocating for* the people to whom we were providing our 'services.' Although well-intentioned, there were some unstated, taken-for-granted assumptions of this work that I had yet recognized, most notably that there were deficits within the communities where the engagement took place and that the skills and knowledge and expertise that we brought in from the academy would help overcome them.

It is through relationships with others, friends in both the academy and the community, who engage in creative and principled development work, that I have been able to challenge and deconstruct the damaging paradigm where there are community deficits and external experts who advocate for those who experience them. Within these relationships, purposeful storytelling and conversation have been the tools that have helped me grow and learn. This happened when I shared with our co-author Sophie my experience moving to a small Midwestern town where my dad was the new public school superintendent. I shared how there was a Native American community in that otherwise culturally monolithic town and my dad quickly sought to rectify the gerrymandered school-districting patterns that seemed to isolate many of the Native American children and their poor white counterparts in one elementary school. In my telling, my dad recognized the injustice within the system and challenged it. Doing so brought considerable pushback and ire from many of the white people in town and I recalled neighbors across our street refusing to talk to not only my dad, but to my entire family. Sophie listened intently and patiently and then asked one simple, critical question that illuminated for me an essential element of white privilege. She asked, 'but what did the Native American community want at that time?' For me, this question provoked tremendous insight as I grasped for the first time the deeper nature or essence of white privilege. Sophie's question provoked my understanding that my dad had great intentions but was moving to advocate *for* the Native American students and their families. He may have later developed strong relationships with the tribal leadership and many other members of the tribe (as he believed he had), but he could not have done so at that early stage. His instinct, his automatic response, was to jump into the situation without learning about it from the perspectives of those he was advocating for, or even if it was an issue for them at all. He was the expert and he was there to help. Following that epiphany, I didn't love my dad any less, nor did I doubt his beliefs in equity and justice. But I did learn there is a danger within my own conditioned consciousness as a White man, a predilection to jump in with the answers, quick analyses, or burst of expertise that comes from position rather than knowing. There are dangers in advocating *for*, rather than *with* others. It is dangerous and it is disruptive and disrespectful. It disrupts the potential for the development of agency in others and it disrespects the powerful potential individuals and communities have to best overcome their own challenges.

I have carried that lesson close to me as a white ally engaged in the work of community development and activist scholarship. Much of our work in Jacksonville and through the University of North Florida has taken place within Black schools, organizations, and neighborhoods. Most of my sisters and brothers in our local work are Black. The issues and dynamics of power, privilege, and race that Sophie surfaced for my reflection in my dad's story are always at play for me. Not only am I often the only White man working in Black communities, but I occupy a more senior and administrative position within our university and many of our team members are/or have been my students.

While sharing a family story provoked a needed shift in my mind and spirit, as a collective, we embrace practices that exemplify our shared belief that conversations are central and critical pedagogical processes (Guajardo, Guajardo, Janson, & Militello, 2016). It is by talking with each other as a new family, sharing stories, perspectives, and insights that we best create the conditions for each other to develop as learners, teacher, leaders, parents, sisters, and brothers. Just as I had to understand more deeply the nature of white privilege and the damage it can cause to people and communities, we are learning together that we continually need to shed the skin of the institution of the academy and the patriarchal and racist conventions that hold us to rigid roles of professor, student, mentor, and protégé.

Instead, we work through the understanding that we must enter the work and community as family; that we are related through hope and possibility; that we share a democratic and populist commitment to advocating alongside people and communities, rather than for them. Our process of writing this manuscript was also replete with the language of family. We listened to each other express things like, 'Why are we like family? Because family knows your voice because you're there.' Or, 'I know there is interest in me and care for me. This interest feels good and lets me know I can be whomever I want to be.' Or, 'I feel like I can push a little harder, falter a little more often. Because my family has my back.' But as important to our words was the context of our actions. We wrote and learned together in our kitchens and living rooms, through cooking and eating meals, sharing laughter, and naming our truths about each other and our work together.

The art of activist scholarship: family brushstrokes

'The world is indeed one family. Therefore the law of the family should be the law of the world.' – M. K. Gandhi

As activist scholars (*academic activists*), we all have lived through some discomforts both common and unique. The awkwardness of incongruity between who we are and the environments we are in, particularly the world of the academy, has challenged, enlightened, and changed us in irreversible ways. It is through the encouragement and hope we have found, not through the language and conventions of higher education, but through that of the family, that we are emboldened to act. We are beginning to name and challenge the fear, uncertainty, and cognitive dissonance of the changes necessary to engage in righteous work within our community. Part of laying the foundation for our scholar activism has been to document, investigate, and make-meaning from our work so we can better co-create the conditions and the spaces for the people in our community to discover their own answers to their local concerns (Guajardo et al., 2016). Furthermore, the individual lived experiences within our (essay authors) group continue to be sources of wisdom and strength as we strive to model family in our university and community.

Our early career experiences (corporate, education, and 'village' neighborhoods) began to frame our understanding of what it means to privilege relationship building in our various spaces and have fueled our need to act morally and ethically on behalf of the oppressed. As products and eventual stewards of public schools, we all chose, optimistically, education as a profession with hopes of making a significant impact. However, we transitioned out of service in public schools with a sense that more can, and should be done to ensure that public schooling becomes more equitable for all students. We also share rich educative and community experiences, which extended beyond institutional walls and have guided our paths to community activism.

The context of our lives and work in a southern, highly segregated, urban hub that still bears vestiges of America's painful legacy of racism behooves us to critically assess how we perpetuate or dismantle inequitable systems in our engagement among each other and within the academy. Prior to our (essay authors') homecoming as scholar activists, our respective sociocultural identities and academic roles may have led us to engage in the same *places* within academia and community for seemingly common causes, but predispose us to work in siloed spaces within these same systems due to socially constructed narratives about our distinct identities. The blend of our racial, gender, and social identities would dictate estrangement from each other if we remain within the traditional fences of the academy. However, our collective narrative provides a glimpse into how the academy can position itself alongside the communities it serves and become an inclusive space for more voices.

In light of the cultural roots of the academy and our country's racial history, the possibility that a *homecoming* can be experienced collectively by a Black woman, two Black men, and a White man in America represents hope and hints at redemption. We find that scholar activism lends itself to a degree of vulnerability, inviting us to reflect often and deeply about the spaces of privilege and historical marginalization that may predispose the groups from which we are born into from working more authentically in academia and within communities. Chris and I have ongoing conversations about the spaces in which we are privileged and how to leverage our influences to further the work in the academy and our collective leadership within the community. Examples of our conversations, and ensuing activism, may include Chris acknowledging his privilege as a White man in the academy, while advocating with me as an untenured Black woman and faculty member. My lived experiences as a Black woman, having been raised in mostly low-income communities, have informed our collective work, providing Chris insight, as appropriate, into the Black communities that he has committed to in his scholarship and teaching practices. Similar conversations and analyses occur among the four of us, as we try to make meaning and overcome the barriers related to our Blackness, Whiteness, genders, and other social statuses to re-imagine a more equitable academy and healthier community. In pursuit of congruence between our shared values and action, scholar activism is the home that draws us out of estrangement and reminds us that we are, indeed, family.

With relationship and family as our central axiom, we seek to use the academy, rather than be used by it in order to build healthier families, organizations, and communities. With a shared belief that the academy should be a space where we all flourish, we have found this can only be done within and through 'family.' Ours is a beautiful painting of family, much more nuanced and textured than the hegemonic Rockwell. Our family life involves crossing boundaries in order to enrich the development and educational processes that nurture us and those we work with in our neighborhoods, organizations, and schools (Guajardo et al., 2016). Our familial relationships transcend existing sociocultural differences and transactional interactions to deepen the impact and influence we have on each other. In doing so, we are growing in our understanding that we are modeling for others within both our university and our community. We are presenting new stories for how scholars and activists can learn, lead, and grow together. This new narrative is not framed around the inflexible hierarchies our institutions and systems often demand. Instead, we seek to understand our work and our relationships through a more universal, generous, and deeper source: the family. These are homecoming stories.

Disclosure statement

No potential conflict of interest was reported by the authors.

References

Buechner, F. (1973). *Wishful thinking: A theological ABC*. New York, NY: Harper & Row.
D'Souza, R. (2014). What can activist scholars learn from Rumi? *Philosophy East & West, 64*(1), 1–24.
Guajardo, M. A., Guajardo, F. J., & del Carmen Casaperalta, E. (2008). Transformative education: Chronicling a pedagogy for social change. *Anthropology & Education Quarterly, 39*, 3–22.

Guajardo, M. A., Guajardo, F. J., Janson, C., & Militello, M. (2016). *Reframing community partnerships in education: Uniting the power of place and wisdom of people*. New York, NY: Routledge.

McKnight, J., & Block, P. (2012). *The abundant community: Awakening the power of families and neighborhoods*. San Francisco, CA: Berrett-Koehler Publishers.

Rodino-Colocino, M. (2012). Participant activism: Exploring a methodology for scholar-activists through lessons learned as a precarious labor organizer. *Communication, Culture and Critique, 5*, 541–562.

Siplon, P. D. (2014). Once you know, you are responsible: The road from scholar to activist. *Journal of Health Politics, Policy and Law, 39*, 483–489.

Index

www.ingramcontent.com/pod-product-compliance
Ingram Content Group UK Ltd.
Pitfield, Milton Keynes, MK11 3LW, UK
UKHW010021280225
455677UK00023B/728

9 780367 264734